Over 130 Favorites
Arranged for Children's Voices
by Larry Haron

Revised! Now Features Nine Musical Scripts
by Karla Worley!

COMPANION MATERIALS

Singalong Book*	301 0074 360
Accompanist Edition	301 0075 367
Vol. 1 Cassette**	701 9274 501
Vol. 1 Compact Disc**	701 9274 595
Vol. 2 Cassette**	701 9724 507
Vol. 2 Compact Disc**	701 9724 590

*The Singalong Book contains the melody and lyrics.
**All recordings are in the Split-Track format. The left channel is the instrumental track, and the right channel includes the vocals. Volume 1 contains 33 songs, Volume 2 contains 30 songs. These are also the songs utilized by the nine musicals in the back of this book.

Art Design by Eddy Design & Illustration
Music Engraving by Brent Roberts
Edited by Ken Barker

WORD MUSIC

Printed by Davis Brothers Publishing Co., Inc., Waco, TX

F O R E W O R D

GREAT SONGS FOR GOD'S KIDS is more than a K–6th grade songbook. **GREAT SONGS** is a rich mixture of the classic songs that children like to sing, plus choice new songs mixed in. The six categories of more than 130 carefully chosen songs and special features make it a must collection for churches, schools and homes.

Contemporary inspirational songs, praise and worship songs or choruses, Scripture songs, classic children's songs, hymns, and seasonal/special day songs give this songbook a unique breadth and variety that makes it ideal for Sunday school, children's choir use, children's church, camp, VBS, private schools, and private home or car use.

Nine excellent mini-musicals scripted by Karla Worley are included in the Accompanist Edition. The first four scripts utilize all of the songs on the Volume One recording. These songs are the first 33 songs in the book, in proper sequence to use for the mini-musicals, just as they are on the recording. The last five scripts utilize most of the songs on the Volume Two recording. The songs are in the proper sequence for musical use on the recording, but not in the book. The following two pages list all of the songs in the nine mini-musicals, and their song number in the book, for easy reference. The musicals are designed to fit within a typical service with minimal preparation. They could even be performed at camp or in a large living room! Following is a brief description of the nine mini-musicals.

Volume One recording:
The Amazin' Praise 'n' Worship Quiz: Welcome to **The Amazin' Praise 'n' Worship Quiz.** Your host, P.W. Singer and his assistant, Little David, lead you in songs, questions, and crazy stunts that will have you laughing and learning about the amazing world of praising.

Parent's Night: Mrs. Lunn is rehearsing the VBS classes for their Parent's Night program. Through the scenes in the program, the children tell the Bible stories they have learned that week. All is not going as Mrs. Lunn planned! Will the program be ready? Join us for a not-so-perfect dress rehearsal.

Show and Tell: Kelsey is excited because she just became a Christian and she can't wait to go to school and tell her friends. But during "Show and Tell" time, Kelsey learns that it's not enough to tell people about the difference Christ makes in your heart; you also have to show them.

Christ the Lord Is Risen Today: Mrs. Stark's Sunday school class has come Easter morning with Easter baskets. Mrs. Stark filled her basket full of unusual Easter symbols. She explains each one and the children make the symbols for their baskets, learning that there is more to Easter than eggs and bunnies.

Volume Two recording:

In the Lord's Army: Billy, a boy of about 7, loves to play soldier; in fact, he imagines it would be great to be a soldier. He even prays about it at bedtime one night, and gets a surprising visit from an angel, with a message from the Commander-in-Chief. Billy is about to get his first assignment as a soldier in God's army, and it is not at all what he expected. By listening in on Billy's conversation with the messenger, we learn how we can have a part in advancing God's kingdom.

Dear God: Mrs. McMinn is teaching her Sunday school class about prayer. She has asked them to keep a prayer journal for a week; each day they are to write down their prayers to God, as if writing a letter to Him. In this script, we eavesdrop on some of the children's letters.

Cheerleading Practice: Tiffany's family has just moved to a new town, and it's their first day unpacking in their new house. Tiffany is alone in her new room, filled with boxes, feeling discouraged and missing her old friends. As she unpacks, she finds encouragement from a surprising source—the Bible. Tiffany learns (and so do we) the power of the Word to encourage us and remind us of God's love and care.

Nature Walk: Mrs. Crosby's choir is on a nature walk; but Ashley and Darren just aren't into it. They think it's boring, and don't see what it has to do with singing. When they decide to sit it out, they get a surprising lesson from nature, and we discover some reasons for praising God.

The Keys to the Kingdom: In this brief service, we take a look at the "keys to the kingdom"; the Beatitudes.

The recorded songs will be fun for kids to perform, to use year-round, or to just enjoy listening to at home. We hope you will enjoy **GREAT SONGS FOR GOD'S KIDS** for years to come!

Larry Haron, Bob Singleton

SONGS ON THE VOL. 1 RECORDING & IN THE BOOK

IN ORDER OF PERFORMANCE

1. THE AMAZIN' PRAISE 'N' WORSHIP QUIZ (MUSICAL #1)

We're Singing Praises . . . SONG NUMBER 1

Amen, Praise the Lord 2

I Will Sing of the Mercies 3

O for a Thousand Tongues 4

Clap Your Hands 5

Rejoice in the Lord Always 6

My God Is So Great,

So Strong and So Mighty 7

To God Be the Glory 8

2. PARENT'S NIGHT (MUSICAL #2)

The B-I-B-L-E 9

Father Abraham 10

Arky, Arky 11

How Did Moses Cross

the Red Sea 12

Ten Commandments Song 13

Only a Boy Named David 14

Zaccheus 15

Give Thanks 16

Thy Word 17

3. SHOW AND TELL (MUSICAL #3)

Born Again 18

This Little Light of Mine 19

Stop! and Let Me Tell You

(Stop-Go-Watch) 20

I Am a C-H-R-I-S-T-I-A-N 21

Jesus Loves Me 22

Into My Heart 23

If You're Happy and You

Know It 24

Blessed Assurance 25

4. CHRIST THE LORD IS RISEN TODAY (MUSICAL #4)

He Lives 26

Behold, What Manner of Love . . 27

Ho-ho-ho-hosanna 28

When I Survey

the Wondrous Cross 29

There Is a Savior 30

Christ Arose 31

He Is Lord 32

Christ the Lord Is Risen Today . 33

SONGS ON THE VOL. 2 RECORDING & IN THE BOOK
IN ORDER OF PERFORMANCE

1. IN THE LORD'S ARMY
(MUSICAL #5)

I'm in the Lord's Army.. SONG NUMBER 45

Beloved 87

Amazing Grace 69

O, How I Love Jesus 125

No Way! We Are Not Ashamed 128

My Turn Now 67

What a Mighty God We Serve. .122

2. DEAR GOD
(MUSICAL #6)

Say to the Lord, "I Love You" . . . 114

God Is So Good 79

Love Him in the Morning 107

Jesus, Name above All Names . 50

Awesome God 78

3. CHEERLEADING PRACTICE
(MUSICAL #7)

Children, Children 35

Do You See What Esau Saw? . . .88

Cast Your Burden 123

His Strength Is Perfect 43

The Joy of the Lord 42

4. NATURE WALK
(MUSICAL #8)

Joyful, Joyful, We Adore Thee . . 96

Hallelu, Hallelujah! 62

The Ducks Go By 38

The Butterfly Song 63

Fairest Lord Jesus 53

He Is Exalted 54

5. THE KEYS TO THE KINGDOM
(MUSICAL #9)

Happy All the Time 52

Seek Ye First 108

Like a River Glorious 80

When I Get to Heaven 65

CONTENTS

IN ALPHABETICAL ORDER

SONG
NUMBER

All Hail, King Jesus 82
All Hail the Power of Jesus' Name 71
Amazing Grace * 69
Amen, Praise the Lord * 2
America, the Beautiful 113
And He Died for All (II Corinthians 5:15) 48
Angels We Have Heard on High 102
Arky, Arky * 11
Away in a Manger 100
Awesome God * 78
Be Exalted, O God 81
Because He Lives 58
Behold, What Manner of Love * 27
Beloved (I John 4: 7-8) * 87
The B-I-B-L-E * 9
Bless His Holy Name 72
Blessed Assurance * 25
Born Again * 18
The Butterfly Song
   (If I Were a Butterfly) * 63
Cast Your Burden * 123
Children, Children * 35
Christ Arose * 31
Christ the Lord Is Risen Today * 33
Clap Your Hands * 5
Come On, Ring Those Bells 97
The Countdown Song 130
Crown Him with Many Crowns 118
Do You See What Esau Saw? * 88
The Ducks Go By * 38
Emmanuel 95
Fairest Lord Jesus * 53
Father Abraham * 10
Father, I Adore You 73
Friends 90
Give Thanks * 16
Glorify Thy Name 37

Go, Tell It on the Mountain 101
God Is a Spirit 83
God Is So Good * 79
Good Christian Kids, Rejoice 99
Great Is the Lord 104
Great Is Thy Faithfulness 119
The Greatest Thing 47
Hallelu, Hallelujah! * 62
Happy All the Time * 52
Happy Re-Birthday 105
Hark! the Herald Angels Sing 92
He Is Exalted * 54
He Is Lord * 32
He Lives * 26
His Name Is Wonderful 40
His Strength Is Perfect * 43
Ho-ho-ho-hosanna * 28
How Did Moses Cross the Red Sea * 12
How Great Thou Art 77
How Majestic Is Your Name 89
I Am a C-H-R-I-S-T-I-A-N * 21
I Am a Promise 66
I Exalt Thee 110
I Just Wanna Be a Sheep * 86
I Live 57
I Love You, Lord 116
I Sing Praises 106
I Surrender All 36
I Will Bless the Lord 126
I Will Call upon the Lord 131
I Will Enter His Gates
   (He Has Made Me Glad) 68
I Will Make You Fishers of Men 51
I Will Sing of the Mercies * 3
If You're Happy and You Know It * 24
I'll Be a Sunbeam 34
I'm in the Lord's Army * 45

* Songs recorded on cassette and compact disc.

CONTENTS
IN ALPHABETICAL ORDER

SONG NUMBER

In His Presence 61
In Moments Like These 117
In My Life, Lord, Be Glorified 121
Into My Heart * 23
Jesus Is Lord of All 127
Jesus Loves 76
Jesus Loves Me * 22
Jesus Loves the Little Children * 75
Jesus, Name above All Names * 50
The Joy of the Lord * 42
Joy to the World ! 93
Joyful, Joyful, We Adore Thee * 96
King of Kings 91
Like a River Glorious * 80
Love Him in the Morning (All Day Song) * 107
Majesty 64
Make Your Dad Glad 132
Mansion Builder 44
My Country, 'Tis of Thee 111
My God Is So Great, So Strong and So Mighty * 7
My Jesus, I Love Thee 109
My Turn Now * 67
No Way! We Are Not Ashamed * 128
O Come, All Ye Faithful 94
O for a Thousand Tongues * 4
O, How I Love Jesus * 125
O the Blood of Jesus * 70
Once in Royal David's City 98
Only a Boy Named David * 14
Open Our Eyes, Lord 56
Our God Reigns 115
Praise the Name of Jesus 55
Redeemed 59
Rejoice in the Lord Always * 6
Rise Again 60
Say to the Lord, "I Love You" * 114
Seek Ye First * 108

Shine Down 85
Shout Hosanna 120
Silent Night 103
Stop! and Let Me Tell You (Stop-Go-Watch) * 20
Surely Goodness and Mercy 39
Sweet Song of Salvation 124
Ten Commandments Song * 13
There Is a Savior * 30
This Is the Day 129
This Little Light of Mine * 19
Thou Art Worthy 41
Through It All 49
Thy Loving Kindness 74
Thy Word * 17
To God Be the Glory * 8
Victory in Jesus 46
We Will Glorify 84
We're Singing Praises * 1
What a Mighty God We Serve * 122
When I Get to Heaven * 65
When I Survey the Wondrous Cross * 29
Zaccheus * 15

VOLUME 1 RECORDING:
The Amazin' Praise 'n' Worship Quiz
    (musical script #1) . . . . page no. 181
Parent's Night (musical script #2) . . . . page no. 189
Show and Tell (musical script #3) . . . . page no. 203
Christ the Lord Is Risen Today
    (musical script #4) . . . . page no. 211
VOLUME 2 RECORDING:
In the Lord's Army (musical script #5) . . . . page no. 222
Dear God (musical script #6) . . . . page no. 237
Cheerleading Practice (musical script #7) . page no. 244
Nature walk (musical script #8) . . . . page no. 252
The Keys to the Kingdom
    (musical script #9) . . . . page no. 261

* Songs recorded on cassette and compact disc.

CATEGORICAL INDEX

CHILDREN'S SONGS

Amen, Praise the Lord*, 2
Arky, Arky *, 11
The B-I-B-L-E *, 9
Born Again *, 18
The Butterfly Song (If I Were a Butterfly) *, 63
Cast Your Burden *, 123
Children, Children * , 35
The Countdown Song , 130
Do You See What Esau Saw? *, 88
The Ducks Go By *, 38
Father Abraham *, 10
Hallelu, Hallelujah! *, 62
Happy All the Time *, 52
Happy Re-Birthday, 105
Ho-ho-ho-hosanna *, 28
How Did Moses Cross the Red Sea *, 12
I Am a C-H-R-I-S-T-I-A-N *, 21
I Am a Promise, 66
I Just Wanna Be a Sheep *, 86

I Will Make You Fishers of Men, 51
If You're Happy and You Know It *, 24
I'll Be a Sunbeam, 34
I'm in the Lord's Army *, 45
Into My Heart *, 23
Jesus Loves, 76
Jesus Loves Me *, 22
Jesus Loves the Little Children *, 75
Love Him in the Morning *, 107
   (All Day Song)
Make Your Dad Glad, 132
My God Is So Great, So Strong and So Mighty *, 7
Only a Boy Named David *, 14
Say to the Lord, "I Love You," * 114
Stop! and Let Me Tell You (Stop-Go-Watch) *, 20
This Little Light of Mine *, 19
We're Singing Praises *, 1
When I Get to Heaven * , 65
Zaccheus *, 15

CONTEMPORARY INSPIRATIONAL CHORUSES

Because He Lives, 58
Friends, 90
His Strength Is Perfect *, 43
In His Presence, 61
Mansion Builder, 44
My Turn Now *, 67

No Way! We Are Not Ashamed *, 128
Rise Again, 60
Shine Down, 85
Sweet Song of Salvation, 124
There Is a Savior *, 30
Through It All, 49

HYMNS

All Hail the Power of Jesus' Name, 71
Amazing Grace *, 69
Blessed Assurance *, 25
Fairest Lord Jesus *, 53
Great Is Thy Faithfulness, 119
How Great Thou Art, 77
I Surrender All, 36
Joyful, Joyful, We Adore Thee *, 96

Like a River Glorious *, 80
My Jesus, I Love Thee, 109
O for a Thousand Tongues *, 4
O, How I Love Jesus *, 125
Redeemed, 59
To God Be the Glory *, 8
Victory in Jesus, 46

* Songs recorded on cassette and compact disc.

PRAISE & WORSHIP SONGS OR CHORUSES

All Hail, King Jesus, 82
Awesome God *, 78
Father, I Adore You, 73
Give Thanks *, 16
Glorify Thy Name, 37
God Is a Spirit, 83
God Is So Good *, 79
Great Is the Lord, 104
The Greatest Thing, 47
He Is Exalted *, 54
He Is Lord *, 32
His Name Is Wonderful, 40
I Exalt Thee, 110
I Live, 57
I Love You, Lord, 116

I Sing Praises, 106
I Will Enter His Gates, 68
   (He Has Made Me Glad)
In Moments Like These, 117
In My Life, Lord, Be Glorified, 121
Jesus Is Lord of All, 127
Jesus, Name above All Names *, 50
King of Kings, 91
Majesty, 64
O the Blood of Jesus *, 70
Open Our Eyes, Lord, 56
Our God Reigns, 115
Praise the Name of Jesus, 55
We Will Glorify, 84
What a Mighty God We Serve *, 122

SCRIPTURE SONGS

And He Died for All, 48
   (II Corinthians 5:15)
Be Exalted, O God, 81
   (Psalm 57:9-11)
Behold, What Manner of Love *, 27
   (I John 3:1)
Beloved (Let Us Love One Another) *, 87
   (I John 4: 7-8)
Bless His Holy Name, 72
   (Psalm 103:1)
Clap Your Hands *, 5
   (Psalm 47:1)
How Majestic Is Your Name, 89
   (Psalm 8:1)
I Will Bless the Lord , 126
   (Psalms 145:1-2, 8-9,17)
I Will Call upon the Lord, 131
   (Psalm 18:3,46)
I Will Sing of the Mercies*, 3
   (Psalm 89:1)

The Joy of the Lord *, 42
   (Nehemiah 8:10; Isaiah 61:1-2; John 4:14)
Rejoice in the Lord Always *, 6
   (Philippians 4:4)
Seek Ye First *, 108
   (Matthew 6:33; 7:7)
Surely Goodness and Mercy, 39
   (Psalm 23:6)
Ten Commandments Song *, 13
   (Based on Exodus 20:4-17;
   Deuteronomy 5:6-21)
This Is the Day, 129
   (Psalm 118:24)
Thou Art Worthy, 41
   (Revelation 4:11)
Thy Loving Kindness, 74
   (Psalm 63:3-4)
Thy Word *, 17
   (Psalm 119:105)

SEASONAL/SPECIAL DAY SONGS
CHRISTMAS

Angels We Have Heard on High, 102
Away in a Manger, 100
Come On, Ring Those Bells, 97
Emmanuel, 95
Go, Tell It on the Mountain, 101
Good Christian Kids, Rejoice, 99
Hark! the Herald Angels Sing, 92
Joy to the World!, 93
O Come, All Ye Faithful, 94
Once in Royal David's City, 98
Silent Night, 103

PATRIOTIC

America, the Beautiful, 113
I Am Thankful to Be an American, 112
My Country, 'Tis of Thee, 111

EASTER

Christ Arose *, 31
Christ the Lord Is Risen Today *, 33
Crown Him with Many Crowns, 118
He Lives *, 26
Shout Hosanna, 120
When I Survey the Wondrous Cross *, 29

* Songs recorded on cassette and compact disc.

We're Singing Praises

Words and Music by
ERNIE RETTINO and DEBBIE KERNER RETTINO
Arr. by Larry Haron

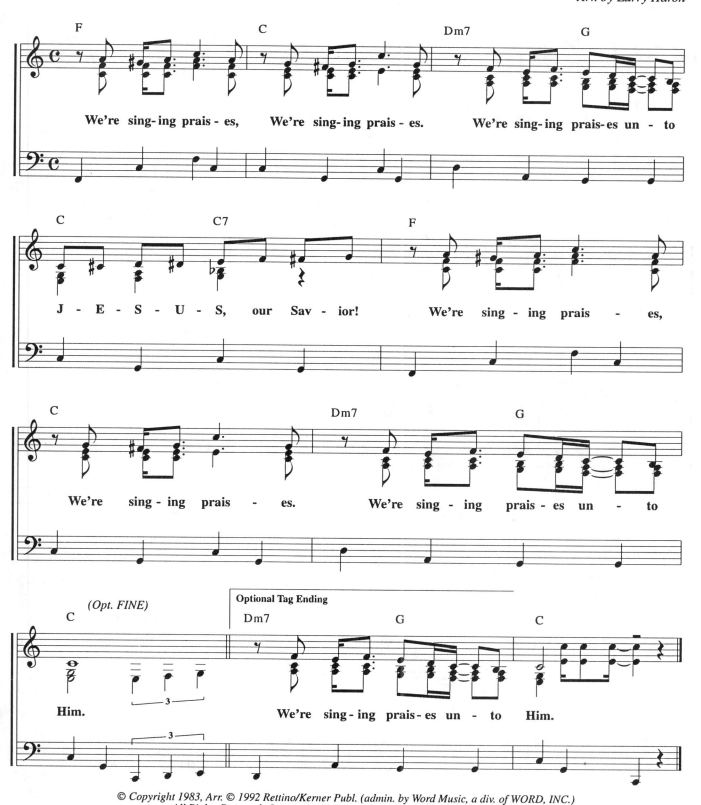

Amen, Praise the Lord

Words and Music by
DEBBIE KERNER RETTINO
Arr. by Larry Haron

*Optional Tag Ending starts here.

2. Marvel not, ye must be born again.
   Marvel not, ye must be born again.
   Marvel not, ye must be born again.

3. Suffer ye the little children to come unto Me.
   Suffer ye the little children to come unto Me.
   And forbid them not, for of such is the Kingdom of Heaven.

I Will Sing of the Mercies

From Psalm 89:1

JAMES H. FILLMORE
Arr. by Larry Haron

faith-ful-ness to all gen-er - a - tions. I will sing of the mer-cies of the

Lord for-e-ver, I will sing of the mer-cies of the Lord.

4   O for a Thousand Tongues

CHARLES WESLEY

CARL G. GLAZER
Arr. by Larry Haron

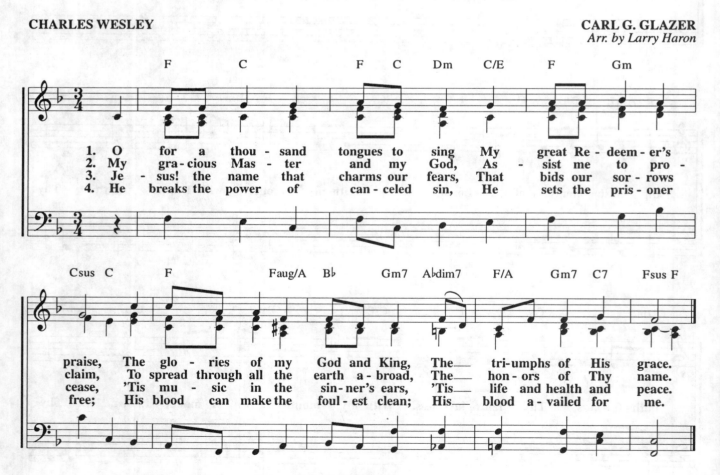

1. O for a thou - sand tongues to sing My great Re - deem - er's
2. My gra - cious Mas - ter and my God, As - sist me to pro -
3. Je - sus! the name that charms our fears, That bids our sor - rows
4. He breaks the power of can - celed sin, He sets the pris - oner

praise, The glo - ries of my God and King, The— tri-umphs of His grace.
claim, To spread through all the earth a - broad, The— hon-ors of Thy name.
cease, 'Tis mu - sic in the sin-ner's ears, 'Tis— life and health and peace.
free; His blood can make the foul-est clean; His— blood a - vailed for me.

Clap Your Hands

5

Based on Psalm 47:1

JIMMY OWENS
Arr. by Larry Haron

6 Rejoice in the Lord Always

Philippians 4:4

TRADITIONAL
Arr. by Larry Haron

My God Is So Great, So Strong and So Mighty

TRADITIONAL
Arr. by Larry Haron

8

To God Be the Glory

FANNY J. CROSBY

WILLIAM H. DOANE
Arr. by Larry Haron

1. To God be the glo - ry, great things He hath done, So
*2. O per - fect re - demp - tion, the pur - chase of blood, To
3. Great things He hath taught us, great things He hath done, And

loved He the world that He gave us His Son, Who yield - ed His
ev - 'ry be - liev - er the prom - ise of God; The vil - est of -
great our re - joic - ing thro' Je - sus the Son; But pur - er and

life an a - tone - ment for sin, And o - pened the
fend - er who tru - ly be - lieves, That mo - ment from
high - er, and great - er will be Our won - der, our

Life - gate that all may go in.
Je - sus a par - don re - ceives. } Praise the Lord, praise the
trans - port, when Je - sus we see.

Verse 2 not included on recording.

9 The B-I-B-L-E

TRADITIONAL
Arr. by Larry Haron

The B - I - B - L - E, yes, that's the book for me. I stand a - lone on the Word of God. The B - I - B - L - E!

Optional transition and higher key
a little faster

The B - I - B - L - E, yes, that's the book for me. I stand a - lone on the Word of God. The B - I - B - L - E!

The Singer's Book does not contain the transition or the higher key.

Father Abraham

TRADITIONAL
Arr. by Larry Haron

Fa-ther A-bra-ham had man-y sons, Man-y sons had Fa-ther

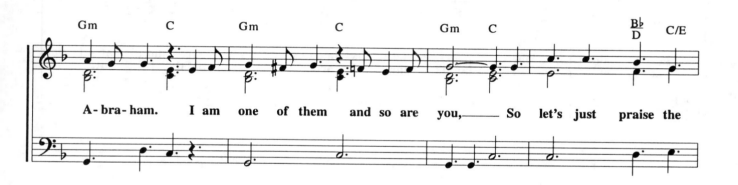

A-bra-ham. I am one of them and so are you,___ So let's just praise the

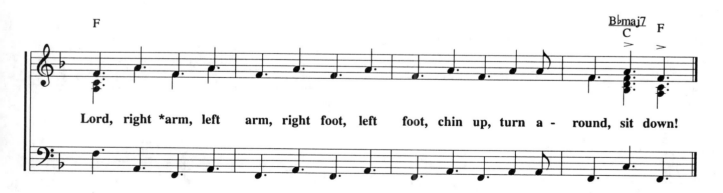

Lord, right *arm, left arm, right foot, left foot, chin up, turn a-round, sit down!

*1st time thru, repeat to beginning at this point, starting a continuous right arm swaying motion. 2nd time, repeat after "left arm," 3rd time after "right foot," etc. Each time, the new part of the body mentioned should start a continuous motion, adding to the other motions.

11

Arky, Arky

TRADITIONAL
Arr. by Larry Haron

rise___ and shine,___ and give God the glo - ry, glo - ry, rise and shine, and

give God the glo - ry, glo - ry, chil - dren___ of the Lord.

3. The animals, the animals, they came in by twosies, twosies,
   Animals, the animals, they came in by twosies, twosies,
   Elephants and kangaroosies, roosies,
   Children of the Lord!

4. It rained and poured for forty daysies, daysies,
   Rained and poured for forty daysies, daysies,
   Almost drove those animals crazies, crazies,
   Children of the Lord!

   Repeat Chorus

5. The sun came out and dried up the landy, landy,
   (Looks there's the sun!) It dried up the landy, landy,
   Everything was fine and dandy, dandy,
   Children of the Lord!

   Repeat Chorus

12

How Did Moses Cross the Red Sea

Words and Music by
HUGH MITCHELL and J.C. BRUMFIELD
Arr. by Larry Haron

Recording contains Tag Ending from here to end.

13 Ten Commandments Song

LARRY HARON
Arr. by Larry Haron

Based on The Ten Commandments

1. You shall not have an - y gods be - fore Me,
(2.) par - ents al - so de - serve your hon - or,
(3.) shall not, shall not com - mit a - dult - ery,

not in an - y shape or form.
there are good things if you will.
nor steal an - y - thing at all,

My name must not be spo - ken light - ly, and each Sab - bath
Do not let ha - tred make you mur - der; do not let your
Nei - ther shall you bear wit - ness false - ly, and to nev - er

14 Only a Boy Named David

TRADITIONAL
Arr. by Larry Haron

15 Zaccheus

TRADITIONAL
Arr. by Larry Haron

This page has been left blank in order
to prevent awkward page turns.

16 Give Thanks

Words and Music by
HENRY SMITH
Arr. by Larry Haron

Give thanks with a grate-ful heart,— Give thanks to the Ho-ly One;— Give thanks— be-cause He's giv-en— Je-sus Christ, His— Son. Give Son. And now, let the weak say, "I am strong," Let the poor say, "I am rich" be-cause of what the Lord has

done   for____ us;   And   now,   let the   weak say,   "I am

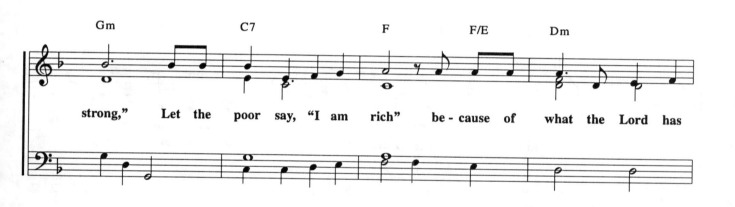

strong,"   Let the   poor say,   "I am   rich"   be - cause of   what the   Lord has

2nd time to CODA⊕   *D.S. al CODA* 𝄋   ⊕ CODA

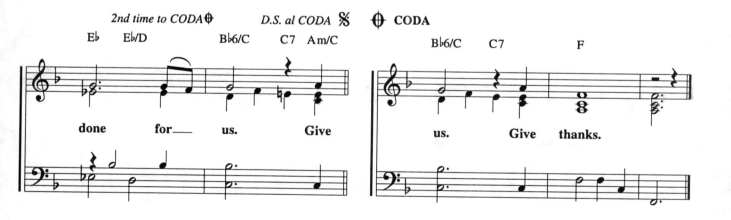

done   for____ us.   Give   us.   Give   thanks.

17 Thy Word

AMY GRANT

MICHAEL W. SMITH
Arr. by Larry Haron

Thy Word is a lamp un-to my feet____ and a light un-to my

path. path. When I feel a-fraid,____ think I've lost my way,____

Still You're there right be-side_____ me. And noth-ing will I fear____ as____

long as You are near,___ Please be near me to the end.___

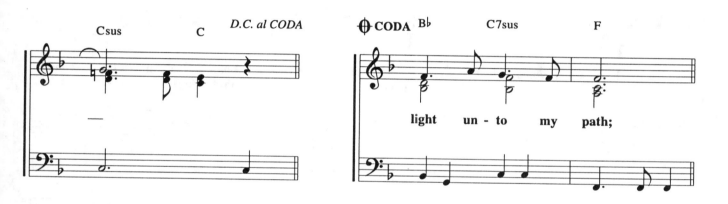

Csus   C   *D.C. al CODA*   ⊕ **CODA** B♭   C7sus   F

light un - to my path;

Optional Tag Ending

mp

F/A   B♭   C7sus   **1.** F   *f* F/A   **2.** F

and a light un - to my path; and a path.

Born Again

Words and Music by
ERNIE RETTINO
Arr. by Larry Haron

19 This Little Light of Mine

TRADITIONAL
Arr. by Larry Haron

This page has been left blank in order
to prevent awkward page turns.

Stop! and Let Me Tell You

(Stop-Go-Watch)

20

Vs. 1 and 2-UNKNOWN
Vs. 3-WALLACE GRANT

UNKNOWN
Arr. by Larry Haron

1. Stop; and let me tell you what the Lord has done for me,
*2. Go; and tell the sto - ry of the Christ of Cal - va - ry,
*3. Watch; and be ye read - y, for the Lord may come to - day.

Stop; and let me tell you what the Lord has done for me. He for -
Go; and tell the sto - ry of the Christ of Cal - va - ry. He'll for -
Watch; and be ye read - y, for the Lord may come to - day. He will

gave my sin and He saved my soul, He cleansed my heart and He made me whole,
give their sins, He will save their souls, He'll cleanse their hearts, He will make them whole,
come a - gain in the clouds for me and take me home for e - ter - ni - ty.

Stop; and let me tell you what the Lord has done for me.
Go; and tell the sto - ry of the Christ of Cal - va - ry.
Watch; and be ye read - y, for the Lord may come to - day.

*Optional verses (not on recording).

21 I Am a C-H-R-I-S-T-I-A-N

TRADITIONAL
Arr. by Larry Haron

Lyrics:

I am a C, I am a C-H, I am a C-H-R-I-S-T-I-A-N; And I have C-H-R-I-S-T in my H-E-A-R-T, and I will

1. L-I-V-E E-T-E-R-N-A-L-L-Y. I am a

2. N-A-L-L-Y.

Jesus Loves Me

ANNA B. WARNER

WILLIAM B. BRADBURY
Arr. by Larry Haron

23 Into My Heart

Words and Music by
HARRY D. CLARKE
Arr. by Larry Haron

In-to my heart, In-to my heart, Come in - to my heart, Lord Je - sus. Come in to - day, come in to stay, Come in - to my heart, Lord Je - sus. Come in - to my heart, Lord Je - sus.

Optional Tag Ending

If You're Happy and You Know It

25 Blessed Assurance

FANNY J. CROSBY

PHOEBE P. KNAPP
Arr. by Larry Haron

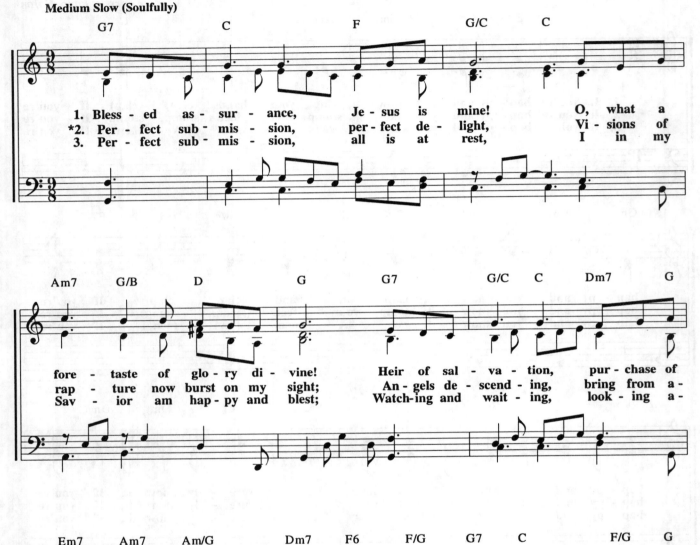

1. Bless - ed as - sur - ance, Je - sus is mine! O, what a
*2. Per - fect sub - mis - sion, per - fect de - light, Vi - sions of
3. Per - fect sub - mis - sion, all is at rest, I in my

fore - taste of glo - ry di - vine! Heir of sal - va - tion, pur - chase of
rap - ture now burst on my sight; An - gels de - scend - ing, bring from a -
Sav - ior am hap - py and blest; Watch-ing and wait - ing, look - ing a -

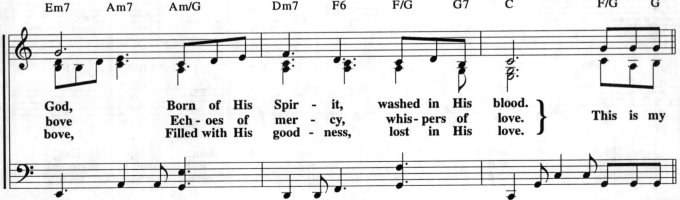

God, Born of His Spir - it, washed in His blood.
bove Ech - oes of mer - cy, whis - pers of love.
bove, Filled with His good - ness, lost in His love. } This is my

Optional verse (not on recording).

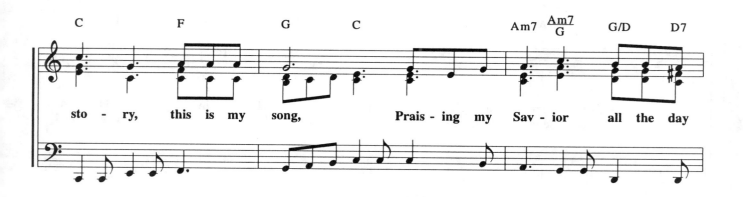

sto - ry, this is my song, Prais - ing my Sav - ior all the day

long; This is my sto - ry, this is my song, Prais - ing my

Optional Tag Ending

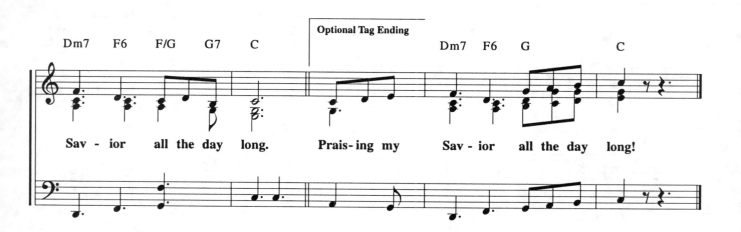

Sav - ior all the day long. Prais - ing my Sav - ior all the day long!

26 He Lives

Words and Music by
ALFRED H. ACKLEY
Arr. by Larry Haron

*1. I serve a ris-en Sav-ior, He's in the world to-day;— I know that He is liv-ing, what-ev-er men may say;— I see His hand of mer-cy, I hear His voice of cheer,— And just the time I need Him,— He's al-ways

2. Re-joice, re-joice, O Christ-ian, lift up your voice and sing— E-ter-nal hal-le-lu-jahs to Je-sus Christ, the King! The Hope of all who seek Him, the Help of all who find,— None oth-er is so lov-ing,— so good and

*If using track, sing only verse one.

*If using track, start here.

27 Behold, What Manner of Love

Words and Music by
PATRICIA VAN TINE
Arr. by Larry Haron

PART I (2-Part Round)

Be - hold, what man-ner of love the Fa-ther has giv-en un-to us,___ Be-

hold, what man-ner of love the Fa-ther has giv-en un-to us,

PART II

that we___ should be called the sons___ of God,

that we___ should be called the sons of God.___

Ho-ho-ho-hosanna

28

TRADITIONAL
Arr. by Larry Haron

*The Singer's Book does not contain the modulation or the higher key.

Arr. © 1992 Word Music (a div. of WORD, INC.)
All Rights Reserved. International Copyright Secured.

29

When I Survey
the Wondrous Cross

ISAAC WATTS

Based on a
GREGORIAN CHANT
Arr. by Larry Haron

1. When I sur-vey the won-drous cross
2. See, from His head, His hands, His feet,
3. Were the whole realm of na-ture mine,

On which the Prince of glo-ry died,
Sor-row and love flow min-gled down;
That were a pre-sent far too small;

My rich-est gain I count but loss,
Did e'er such love and sor-row meet,
Love so a-maz-ing, so di-vine,

And pour con-tempt on all my pride.
Or thorns com-pose so rich a crown?
De-mands my soul, my life, my all.

There Is a Savior

Words and Music by
BOB FARRELL, GREG NELSON
and SANDI PATTI HELVERING
Arr. by Larry Haron

31 Christ Arose

Words and Music by
ROBERT LOWRY
Arr. by Larry Haron

1. Low in the grave He lay, Je-sus my Sav - ior! Wait - ing the
*2. Vain - ly they watch His bed, Je-sus my Sav - ior! Vain - ly they
3. Death can - not keep his prey, Je-sus my Sav - ior! He tore the

com - ing day,
seal the dead, } Je - sus my Lord! Up from the grave He a - rose, With a
bars a - way,

might - y tri - umph o'er His foes; He a - rose a Vic - tor from the

*Optional Verse (not on recording).

dark do-main, And He lives for-e-ver with His saints to reign, He a-

rose! He a-rose! Hal-le-lu-jah! Christ a-rose!

He Is Lord

32

TRADITIONAL
Arr. by Larry Haron

He is Lord, He is Lord! He is ris-en from the dead and He is

Lord! Ev-'ry knee shall bow, ev-'ry tongue con-fess that Je-sus Christ is Lord.

33 Christ the Lord Is Risen Today

CHARLES WESLEY

From *LYRA DAVIDICA*
Arr. by Larry Haron

*Verse 2 is optional (not included on recording).

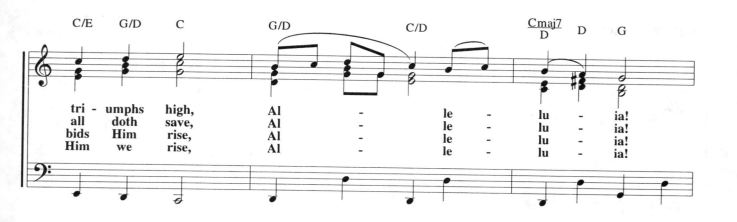

tri - umphs high, Al - le - lu - ia!
all doth save, Al - le - lu - ia!
bids Him rise, Al - le - lu - ia!
Him we rise, Al - le - lu - ia!

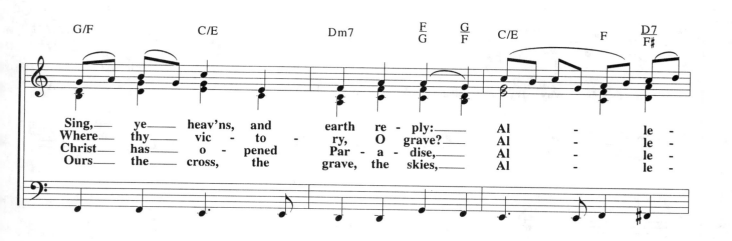

Sing,___ ye heav'ns, and earth re - ply:___ Al - le -
Where___ thy___ vic - to - ry, O grave? Al - le -
Christ___ has___ o - pened Par - a - dise,___ Al - le -
Ours___ the___ cross, the grave, the skies,___ Al - le -

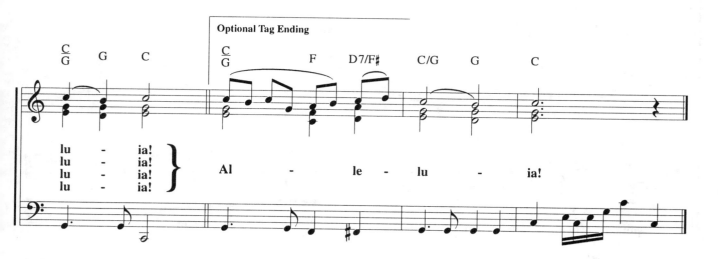

Optional Tag Ending

lu - ia!
lu - ia!
lu - ia!
lu - ia!

Al - le - lu - ia!

34 I'll Be a Sunbeam

NELLIE TALBOT

EDWIN O. EXCELL
Arr. by Larry Haron

Je-sus wants me for a sun-beam, To shine for Him each day;

In ev-'ry way try to please Him, at home, at school, at play.— A

sun-beam, a sun-beam, Je-sus wants me for a sun-beam; A

sun-beam, a sun-beam, I'll be a sun-beam for Him.

Children, Children

35

Words and Music by
ROBERT C. EVANS
Arr. by Larry Haron

Chil - dren, chil - dren, come and lis - ten, come and hear____ of
Chil - dren, chil - dren, come and see____ Him, come and see____ how

Je - sus' love.____ }
Je - sus loves.____ } Chil - dren, chil - dren, come and touch____ Him,

come and touch____ our Bi - ble friend.____ Je - sus, Je - sus,

come and bless____ us, come and bless____ us with Your love.____

36 I Surrender All

JUDSON W. VAN DeVENTER

WINFIELD S. WEEDEN
Arr. by Larry Haron

1. All to Je - sus I sur - ren - der, All to Him I free - ly give;
2. All to Je - sus I sur - ren - der, Make me, Sav - ior, whol - ly Thine;
3. All to Je - sus I sur - ren - der, Lord, I give my - self to Thee;

I will ev - er love and trust Him, In His pres - ence dai - ly live.
May Thy Ho - ly Spir - it fill me, May I know Thy pow'r di - vine.
Fill me with Thy love and pow - er, Let Thy bless - ing fall on me.

I sur - ren - der all, I sur - ren - der all.

All to Thee, my bless - ed Sav - ior, I sur - ren - der all.

Glorify Thy Name

37

Words and Music by
DONNA ADKINS
Arr. by Larry Haron

1. Fa - ther, we love You, we wor - ship and a - dore You,
2. Je - sus, we love You, we wor - ship and a - dore You,
3. Spir - it, we love You, we wor - ship and a - dore You,

Glo - ri - fy Thy name in all the earth.

Glo - ri - fy Thy name, Glo - ri - fy Thy name,

Glo - ri - fy Thy name in all the earth.

The Ducks Go By

38

UNKNOWN
Arr. by Larry Haron

Well, the ducks go by.— (quack, quack, quack, quack) Things go up,— things go down— And the world goes 'round and a-round— and a-round and a-round,— And God lives on.—

1. He made the birds, He made the bees.
2. He died for you, He died for me;

He made the flow'rs and all the trees.— Can't you see
He died to set His peo-ple free— from sin.

39 Surely Goodness and Mercy

Words and Music by
JOHN W. PETERSON and **ALFRED B. SMITH**
Arr. by Larry Haron

40 His Name Is Wonderful

Words and Music by
AUDREY MIEIR
Arr. by Larry Haron

He's the great Shep-herd, the Rock of all a-ges,

Al - might - y God is He;

Bow down be-fore Him, Love and a-dore Him,

His name is Won-der-ful, Je-sus, my Lord.

41 Thou Art Worthy

Words and Music by
PAULINE M. MILLS
Arr. by Larry Haron

The Joy of the Lord

42

Words and Music by
ALLIENE G. VALE
Arr. by Larry Haron

His Strength Is Perfect

43

Words and Music by
STEVEN CURTIS CHAPMAN and JERRY SALLEY
Arr. by Larry Haron

Mansion Builder

Words and Music by
ANNE HERRING
Arr. by Larry Haron

44

I'm in the Lord's Army

TRADITIONAL
Arr. by Larry Haron

I may nev - er march in the in - fan - try, ride in the cav - al - ry,

shoot the ar - til - ler - y. I may nev - er fly o'er the en - e - my, but

2nd (Last) time to CODA

I'm in the Lord's ar - my. I'm in the Lord's ar -

my. I'm in the Lord's ar - my.

D.C. al CODA

CODA

my.

Victory in Jesus

46

Words and Music by
EUGENE M. BARTLETT, SR.
Arr. by Larry Haron

O vic-to-ry in Je-sus, my Sav-ior, for-

ev-er, He sought me and bo't me with His re-deem-ing

blood; He loved me ere I knew Him, and all my love is

due Him, He plunged me to vic-to-ry be-neath the cleans-ing flood.

The Greatest Thing

Words and Music by
MARK PENDERGRASS
Arr. by Larry Haron

48

And He Died for All
(II Corinthians 5:15)

LARRY HARON
Arr. by Larry Haron

Through It All

Words and Music by
ANDRAÉ CROUCH
Arr. by Larry Haron

Through it all,_____ Through it all,_____ I've learned to trust in Je-sus, I've learned to trust in God; Through it all,_____ Through it all,_____ I've learned to de-pend up-on His Word._____

50 Jesus, Name above All Names

Words and Music by
NAIDA HEARN
Arr. by Larry Haron

Je - sus, name a - bove all names, beau - ti - ful Sav - ior, glo - ri - ous Lord. Em - man - u - el, God is with us, bless - ed Re - deem - er, Liv - ing Word.

I Will Make You Fishers of Men 51

Words and Music by
HARRY D. CLARKE
Arr. by Larry Haron

52 Happy All the Time

TRADITIONAL
Arr. by Larry Haron

I'm in-right, out-right, up-right, down-right hap-py all the time, I'm in-right, out-right, up-right, down-right hap-py all the time; When Je-sus Christ came in And cleansed my heart from sin, I'm in-right, out-right, up-right, down-right hap-py all the time.

Fairest Lord Jesus

ANONYMOUS GERMAN HYMN
SOURCE UNKNOWN, stanzas 1-3
JOSEPH A. SEISS, stanza 4

SCHLESISCHE VOLKSLIEDER
Arr. by Larry Haron

1. Fair - est Lord Je - sus, Rul - er of all na - ture, O Thou of God and man the Son:
2. Fair are the mead - ows, Fair - er still the wood - lands, Robed in the bloom - ing garb of spring:
3. Fair is the sun - shine, Fair - er still the moon - light, And all the twin - kling star - ry host:
4. Beau - ti - ful Sav - ior! Lord of the na - tions! Son of God and Son of Man!

Thee will I cher - ish, Thee will I hon - or, Thou my soul's glo - ry, joy, and crown.
Je - sus is fair - er, Je - sus is pur - er, Who makes the woe - ful heart to sing.
Je - sus shines bright - er, Je - sus shines pur - er Than all the an - gels heaven can boast.
Glo - ry and hon - or, Praise, ad - o - ra - tion, Now and for - ev - er - more be Thine!

54 He Is Exalted

Words and Music by
TWILA PARIS
Arr. by Larry Haron

He is ex-alt-ed, the King is ex-alt-ed on high. I will praise Him.

He is ex-alt-ed, for-ev-er ex-alt-ed and I will praise His name.

He is the Lord, for-ev-er His truth shall reign.

Heav-en and earth re-joice in His ho-ly name. He is ex-alt-ed, the

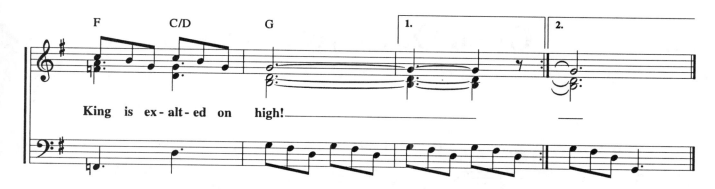

King is ex - alt - ed on high!

Praise the Name of Jesus

55

Words and Music by
ROY HICKS, JR.
Arr. by Larry Haron

Praise the name of Je - sus, Praise the name of Je - sus,

He's my rock, He's my for - tress, He's my de - liv - er - er, in

Him will I trust. Praise the name of Je - sus.

56 Open Our Eyes, Lord

Words and Music by
ROBERT CULL
Arr. by Larry Haron

I Live

57

Words and Music by
RICH COOK
Arr. by Larry Haron

58

Because He Lives

GLORIA GAITHER and WILLIAM J. GAITHER

WILLIAM J. GAITHER
Arr. by Larry Haron

59 Redeemed

FANNY J. CROSBY

A.L. BUTLER
Arr. by Larry Haron

Verse lyrics:

1. Re - deemed, how I love to pro - claim it! Re-
2. Re - deemed, and so hap - py in Je - sus, No -
3. I think of my bless - ed Re - deem - er, I

deemed by the blood of the Lamb; Re - deemed thro' His
lan - guage my rap - ture can tell; I know
think of Him all the day long; I sing, that for

in - fi - nite mer - cy, His child, and for - ev - er, I am. ____ Re-
light of His pres - ence With me doth con - tin - ual - ly dwell. ____
can - not be si - lent; His love is the theme of my song. ____

deemed, ____ re - deemed, ____ Re - deemed by the blood of the Lamb; ____ Re-

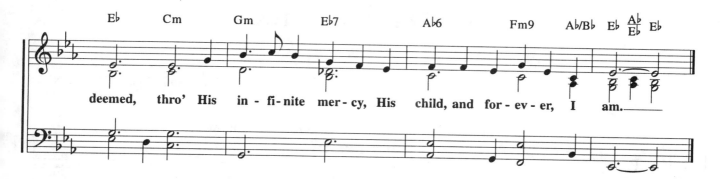

deemed, thro' His in-fi-nite mer-cy, His child, and for-ev-er, I am.

Rise Again

60

Words and Music by
DALLAS HOLM
Arr. by Larry Haron

'Cause I'll rise a-gain;
rise a-gain;
Ain't no pow'r on earth can tie me down;
Ain't no pow'r on earth can keep me back;

Yes, I'll rise a-gain;
Yes, I'll rise a-gain;

Death can't keep me in the ground.
Come to take my peo-ple

'Cause I'll
back.

61
In His Presence

Words and Music by
DICK and MELODIE TUNNEY
Arr. by Larry Haron

Hallelu, Hallelujah!

62

TRADITIONAL
Arr. by Larry Haron

63 The Butterfly Song
(If I Were a Butterfly)

Words and Music by
BRIAN HOWARD
Arr. by Larry Haron

1. If I were a but-ter-fly,___ I'd thank You, Lord, for
2. If I were an el-e-phant,___ I'd thank You, Lord, by
3. If I were a wig-gly worm,___ I'd thank You, Lord, that

giv-ing me wings,___ and if I were a rob-in in a tree, I'd
rais-ing my trunk,___ and if I were a kan-ga-roo,___
I___ could squirm,___ and if I were a croc-o-dile, I'd

thank You, Lord, that I could sing,___ And if I were a
I'd just hop right up to You.___ And if I were an
thank You, Lord, for my big smile.___ And if I were a

fish in the sea,___ I'd wig-gle my tail, and I'd
oc-to-pus,___ I'd thank___ You, Lord, for___
fuz-zy wuz-zy bear, I'd thank___ You, Lord, for my

Majesty

Words and Music by
JACK HAYFORD
Arr. by Larry Haron

64

65 When I Get to Heaven

TRADITIONAL
Arr. by Larry Haron

I Am a Promise

Words and Music by
WILLIAM J. and GLORIA GAITHER
Arr. by Larry Haron

I am a prom- ise, I am a pos- si- bil- i- ty; I am a prom- ise with a cap- i- tal "P,"— I am a great big bun- dle of po- ten- ti- al- i- ty. And I'm a- learn- in' to hear God's voice— and I'm a- try- in'— to make the right choic- es. I'm a

prom - ise to be___ an - y - thing God wants me to be.___

My Turn Now

67

Words and Music by
STEVEN CURTIS CHAPMAN and BRENT LAMB
Arr. by Larry Haron

Well, it's my turn now,___ yes, it's my turn now.___

My turn to give my life a - way.___ Well, it's ___

68

I Will Enter His Gates
(He Has Made Me Glad)

Words and Music by
LEONA VON BRETHORST
Arr. by Larry Haron

He has made me glad, He has made me glad. I will re - joice, for He has made me glad.

He has made me glad, He has made me glad. I will re - joice, for He has made me glad.

69 Amazing Grace

JOHN NEWTON

TRADITIONAL
Arr. by Larry Haron

1. A - maz - ing grace! how sweet the
2. 'Twas grace that taught my heart to
3. Thru man - y dan - gers, toils and
4. When we've been there ten thou - sand

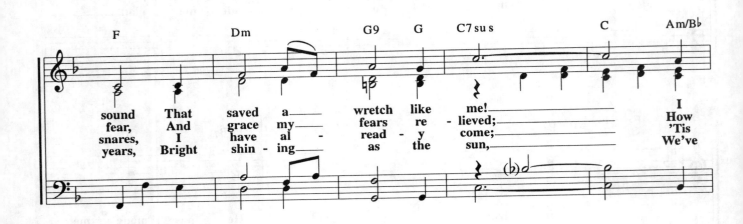

sound, That saved a wretch like me! I
fear, And grace my fears re - lieved; How
snares, I have al - read - y come; 'Tis
years, Bright shin - ing as the sun, We've

once was lost but now am found, Was
pre - cious did that grace ap - pear far, The
grace hath brought me safe thus found, praise And
no less days to sing God's pear, Than

blind   but   now   I   see.
hour   I   first   be - lieved.
grace   will   lead   me   home.
when   we'd   first   be - gun.

O the Blood of Jesus

70

TRADITIONAL
Arr. by Larry Haron

O the blood of Je - sus, O the blood of Je - sus,

O the blood of Je - sus, It wash - es white as snow.

71 All Hail the Power of Jesus' Name

EDWARD PERRONET
Adapted by JOHN RIPPON

JAMES ELLOR
Arr. by Larry Haron

72 Bless His Holy Name

BASED ON PSALM 103

ANDRAÉ CROUCH
Arr. by Larry Haron

Bless the Lord, O my soul, and all that is with-

in me, bless His ho - ly name.

FINE

He has done great things,

He has done great things,_____ He has done great things. Bless His ho - ly name.

D.C. al FINE

Father, I Adore You

73

Words and Music by
TERRYE COELHO
Arr. by Larry Haron

PART I *(May be sung as a 3-part round)*

1. Fa - ther, I a - dore You,   Lay my life be -
2. Je - sus, I a - dore You,   Lay my life be -
3. Spir - it, I a - dore You,   Lay my life be -

PART II

PART III

fore You,   How I love_____ You.
fore You,   How I love_____ You.
fore You,   How I love_____ You.

74   Thy Loving Kindness

Words and Music by
HUGH MITCHELL
Arr. by Larry Haron

Jesus Loves the Little Children

REV. C. H. WOOLSTON

GEORGE F. ROOT
Arr. by Larry Haron

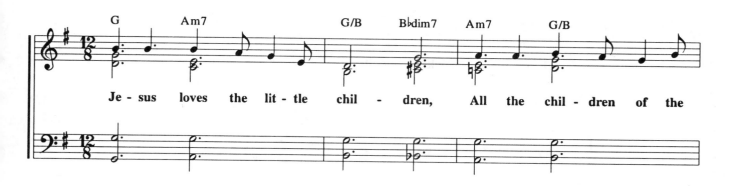

Je - sus loves the lit - tle chil - dren, All the chil - dren of the

world._____ Red and yel - low, black and white, They are

pre - cious in His sight; Je - sus loves the lit - tle chil - dren of the world._____

76

Jesus Loves

ANONYMOUS
Adapted by J.F.

JILL FREEMAN
Arr. by Joseph Linn

How Great Thou Art

Words and Music by
STUART K. HINE
Arr. by Larry Haron

1. O Lord my God, when I in awe-some won-der Con-sid-er
2. And when I think that God, His Son not spar-ing, Sent Him to
3. When Christ shall come with shout of ac-cla-ma-tion And take me

all the worlds Thy hands have made, in, I see the
die, I what scarce can take it my heart! That on the
home, what joy shall fill my Then I shall

stars, I hear the roll-ing thun-der, Thy pow'r thro'
cross, my bur-den glad-ly bear-ing, He bled and
bow in hum-ble ad-o-ra-tion, And there pro-

78 Awesome God

Words and Music by
RICH MULLINS
Arr. by Larry Haron

Our God is an awe-some God; He reigns from

heaven a-bove With wis-dom, pow'r and love. Our God is an awe-some

God! Our God! Our God is an awe-some God! Our

God Is So Good

79

TRADITIONAL
Arr. by Larry Haron

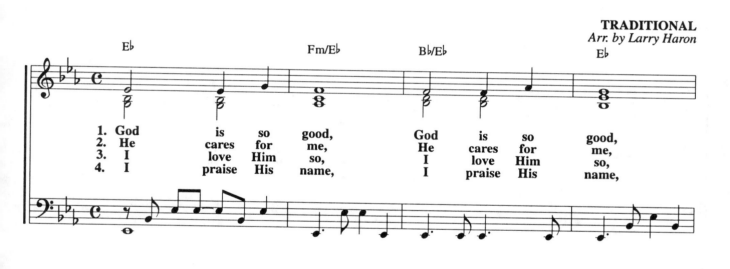

1. God is so good,
2. He cares so for me,
3. I love Him so,
4. I praise His name,

God is so good,
He cares so for me,
I love Him so,
I praise His name,

God is so good, He's so good to me!
He cares for me, He's so good to me!
I love Him so, He's so good to me!
I praise His name, He's so good to me!

80 Like a River Glorious

FRANCES RIDLEY HAVERGAL

JAMES MOUNTAIN
Arr. by Larry Haron

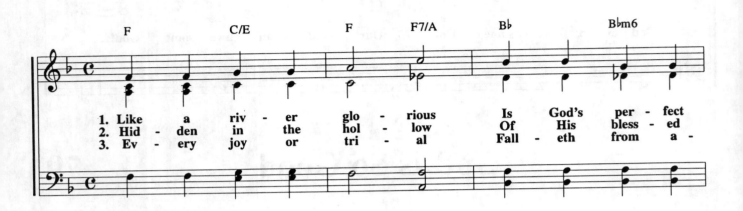

1. Like a riv - er glo - rious Is God's per - fect
2. Hid - den in the hol - low Of His bless - ed
3. Ev - ery joy or tri - al Fall - eth from a -

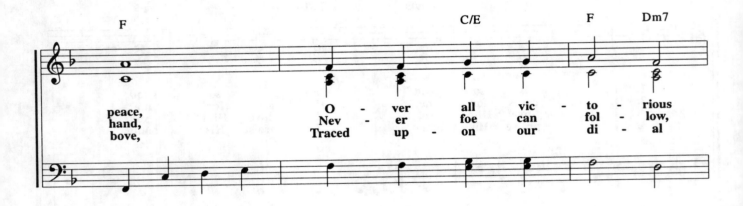

peace, O - ver all vic - to - rious
hand, Nev - er foe can fol - low,
bove, Traced up - on our di - al

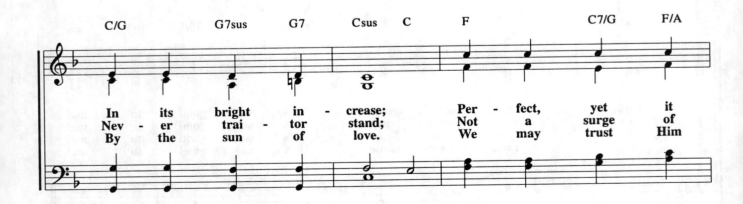

In its bright in - crease; Per - fect, yet it of
Nev - er trai - tor stand; Not a surge of
By the sun of love. We may trust Him

81

Be Exalted, O God
(I Will Give Thanks)

Words and Music by
BRENT CHAMBERS
Arr. by Larry Haron

I will give thanks to Thee, O— Lord, a-mong the peo-ple. I will sing prais-es to Thee a-mong the na-tions.—— For Thy stead-fast love is great, is— great to the heav-ens, and Thy faith-ful-ness, Thy— faith-ful-ness to— the

82 All Hail, King Jesus

Words and Music by
DAVE MOODY
Arr. by Larry Haron

All hail, King Je - sus! _____ All hail, Em -

man - u - el, _____ King of kings, Lord of

lords, Bright Morn - ing Star. _____ And through - out e - ter - ni -

ty, I'm going to praise Him, _____ And for -

ev - er - more   I   will   reign   with   Him._____

God Is a Spirit

83

Westminster Shorter Definition of God

BOB SANDER-CEDERLOF
Arr. by Larry Haron

God   is a spir - it,   in - fi - nite, e - ter - nal,   un - chang - a - ble;   In His

be - ing,   Wis - dom,   Pow - er,   Ho - li - ness,   Jus - tice,   Good - ness and   Truth.

We Will Glorify

Words and Music by
TWILA PARIS
Arr. by Larry Haron

1. We will glo - ri - fy the King of kings, we will glo - ri - fy the Lamb; We will glo - ri - fy Him in Lord of lords, who ___ is the great I AM.

2. Lord Je - ho - vah reigns in maj - es - ty, we will bow be - fore the His throne; We will wor - ship Him a - bove the right - eous - ness, we will wor - ship Him I a - lone.

3. He is Lord of heav - en, Lord of earth, He is Lord of all who live; He is Lord u - ni - verse, all ___ praise to Him we give.

4. Hal - le - lu - jah to the King of kings, hal - le - lu - jah all to the Lamb; Hal - le - lu - jah to the Lord of lords, who ___ is the great I AM.

Shine Down

85

Words and Music by
BILLY SMILEY, MARK GERSMEHL
and BOB FARRELL
Arr. by Larry Haron

86 I Just Wanna Be a Sheep

UNKNOWN
Arr. by Larry Haron

87 Beloved
(I John 4:7-8)

DENNIS RYDER
Arr. by Larry Haron

I JOHN 4: 7-8

With a Calypso feel

Be - lov - ed,___ let us love___ one an - oth - er,___ for love is of God,___ and ev - 'ry - one that lov - eth is born of God,___ and know - eth God.___ He that lov - eth not know - eth not God,___ for God is love.___ Be - lov - ed,___

let us love____ one an-oth-er, First John four: sev-en and eight.____

Do You See What Esau Saw? 88

LARRY HARON

ENGLISH FOLK MELODY
Arr. by Larry Haron

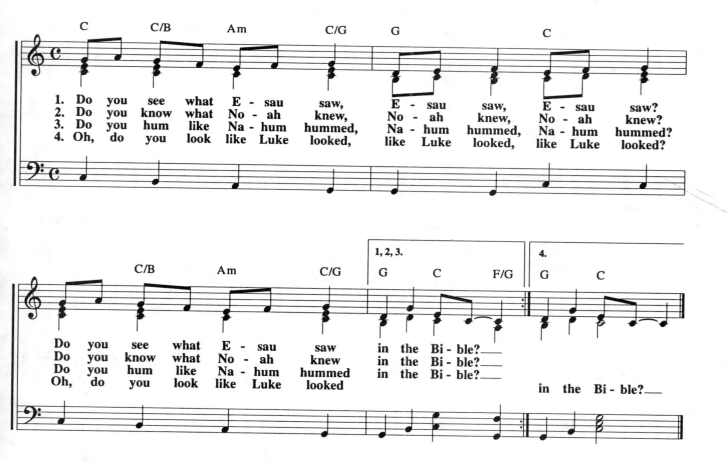

1. Do you see what E-sau saw, E-sau saw, E-sau saw?
2. Do you know what No-ah knew, No-ah knew, No-ah knew?
3. Do you hum like Na-hum hummed, Na-hum hummed, Na-hum hummed?
4. Oh, do you look like Luke looked, like Luke looked, like Luke looked?

Do you see what E-sau saw in the Bi-ble?____
Do you know what No-ah knew in the Bi-ble?____
Do you hum like Na-hum hummed in the Bi-ble?____
Oh, do you look like Luke looked in the Bi-ble?____

89 How Majestic Is Your Name

Words and Music by
MICHAEL W. SMITH

Friends

90

Words and Music by
MICHAEL W. and DEBORAH D. SMITH
Arr. by Larry Haron

91 King of Kings

SOPHIE CONTY and NAOMI BATYA

ANCIENT HEBREW FOLKSONG
Arr. by Larry Haron

PART I *(May be sung as a 2-Part Round.)*

King of kings and Lord of lords, glo - ry, hal - le - lu - jah!

PART II

Repeat and FINE

Je - sus, Prince of Peace, glo - ry, hal - le - lu - jah!

92 Hark! the Herald Angels Sing

CHARLES WESLEY

FELIX MENDELSSOHN
Arr. by Larry Haron

1. Hark! the her - ald an - gels sing, "Glo - ry to the
2. Christ, by high - est heav'n a - dored; Christ, the ev - er -
3. Hail the heav'n-born Prince of Peace! Hail the Sun of

new - born King; Peace on earth, and mer - cy mild,
last - ing Lord! Late in time be - hold Him come,
Right - eous - ness! Light and life to all He brings,

93 Joy to the World!

ISAAC WATTS

GEORGE FREDERICK HANDEL
Arr. by Larry Haron

94 O Come, All Ye Faithful

LATIN HYMN; ascribed to JOHN FRANCIS WADE

JOHN FRANCIS WADE
Arr. by Larry Haron

1. O come, all ye faith-ful, joy-ful and tri-um-phant, O
2. Sing choirs of an-gels, sing in ex-ul-ta-tion,
3. Yea, Lord, we greet Thee, born this hap-py morn-ing,

come ye, O come ye to Beth-le-hem! Come and be-
sing, all ye bright hosts of heav'n a-bove! Glo-ry to
Je-sus, to Thee be all glo-ry giv'n; Word of the

hold Him, born the King of an-gels! } O come, let us a-dore Him, O
God, all glo-ry in the high-est!
Fa-ther, now in flesh ap-pear-ing!

come, let us a-dore Him, O come, let us a-dore Him, Christ the Lord!

Emmanuel

95

Words and Music by
BOB McGEE
Arr. by Larry Haron

Em - man - u - el,_____ Em - man - u - el,_____

___ His name is called_____ Em - man - u - el,

God is with us,_____ re - veal'd in us,_____

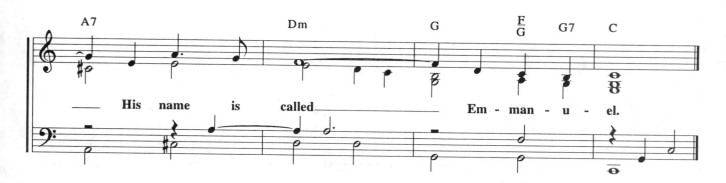

___ His name is called_____ Em - man - u - el.

96 Joyful, Joyful, We Adore Thee

HENRY VAN DYKE

LUDWIG VAN BEETHOVEN
Arr. by Larry Haron

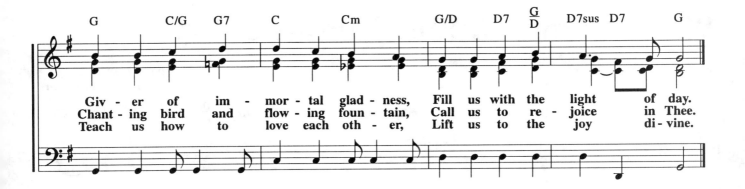

Come On, Ring Those Bells 97

**Words and Music by
ANDREW CULVERWELL**
Arr. by Larry Haron

Come on, ring those bells, light the Christ-mas tree, Je-sus is the King born for you and me. Come on, ring those bells, ev-'ry-bod-y say, "Je-sus, we re-mem-ber this Your birth - day." birth - day."

98 Once in Royal David's City

CECIL F. ALEXANDER

HENRY J. GAUNTLETT
Arr. by Larry Haron

Good Christian Kids, Rejoice   99

LATIN CAROL

GERMAN MELODY
Arr. by Larry Haron

1. Good Chris-tian kids, re-joice With heart and soul and voice;
2. Good Chris-tian kids, re-joice With heart and soul and voice;
3. Good Chris-tian kids, re-joice With heart and soul and voice;

Give ye heed to what we say: News! News! Je-sus Christ is
Now ye hear of end-less bliss: Joy! Joy! Je-sus Christ was
Now ye need not fear the grave: Peace! Peace! Je-sus Christ was

born to-day! Ox and ass be-fore Him bow, And He is in the
born for this! He has o-pened heav-en's door, And man is bless-ed
born to save! Calls you one and calls you all To gain His ev-er-

man-ger now: Christ is born to-day! Christ is born to-day!
ev-er-more: Christ was born for this! Christ was born for this!
last-ing hall: Christ was born to save! Christ was born to save!

100 Away in a Manger

Stanzas 1 and 2, source unknown
JOHN THOMAS McFARLAND, stanza 3

JAMES R. MURRAY
Arr. by Larry Haron

1. A - way in a man - ger, no crib for a
2. The cat - tle are low - ing, the Ba - by a -
3. Be near me, Lord Je - sus, I ask Thee to

bed, The lit - tle Lord Je - sus laid down His sweet
wakes, But lit - tle Lord Je - sus, no cry - ing He
stay Close by me for - ev - er, and love me, I

head; The stars in the sky____ looked down where He
makes, I love Thee, Lord Je - sus, look down from the
pray. Bless all the dear chil - dren in Thy ten - der

lay, The lit - tle Lord Je - sus, a - sleep on the hay.
sky, And stay by my cra - dle till morn - ing is nigh.
care, And fit us for heav - en, to live with Thee there.

Go, Tell It on the Mountain

101

TRADITIONAL SPIRITUAL
Stanzas written by JOHN W. WORK II

TRADITIONAL SPIRITUAL
Arr. by Larry Haron

Go tell it on the moun-tain, O-ver the hills and ev-'ry-where;

Go tell it on the moun-tain That Je-sus Christ is born.
{ 1. While
2. The
3. Down

shep - herds kept their watch - ing O'er si - lent flocks by night, Be -
shep - herds feared and trem - bled When, lo! a - bove the earth Rang
in a low - ly man - ger The hum - ble Christ was born And

hold, through - out the heav - ens There shone a ho - ly light.
out the an - gel cho - rus That hailed our Sav - ior's birth.
God sent us sal - va - tion That bless - ed Christ - mas morn.

102   Angels We Have Heard on High

TRADITIONAL FRENCH CAROL
Arr. by Larry Haron

1. An - gels we have heard on high, Sweet - ly sing - ing o'er the plains,
2. Shep - herds, why this ju - bi - lee? Why your joy - ous strains pro - long?
3. Come to Beth - le - hem, and see Him whose birth the an - gels sing;
4. See with - in a man - ger laid Je - sus, Lord of heav'n and earth!

And the moun - tains in re - ply, Ech - o back their joy - ous strains.
Say what may the ti - dings be, Which in - spire your heav'n - ly song?
Come, a - dore on bend - ed knee Christ the Lord, the new - born King.
Ma - ry, Jo - seph, lend your aid, With us sing our Sav - ior's birth.

Glo - - - - ri - a in ex - cel - sis De - o,

Glo - - - - ri - a in ex - cel - sis De - o.

Silent Night

103

JOSEPH MOHR

FRANZ GRÜBER
Arr. by Larry Haron

1. Si - lent night, ho - ly night, All is calm,
2. Si - lent night, ho - ly night, Shep - herds quake
3. Si - lent night, ho - ly night, Son of God,

all is bright Round yon vir - gin moth - er and Child,
at the sight. Glo - ries stream from heav - en a - far,
love's pure light Ra - diant beams from Thy ho - ly face,

Ho - ly In - fant so ten - der and mild, Sleep in heav - en - ly
heaven - ly hosts sing al - le - lu - ia; Christ the Sav - ior is
With the dawn of re - deem - ing grace, Je - sus, Lord, at Thy

peace, Sleep in heav - en - ly peace.
born! Christ the Sav - ior is born!
birth, Je - sus, Lord, at Thy birth.

104 Great Is the Lord

Words and Music by
MICHAEL W. and DEBORAH D. SMITH
Arr. by Larry Haron

105 Happy Re-Birthday!

Words and Music by
ERNIE RETTINO
Arr. by Larry Haron

*You may substitute another name or other names.

I Sing Praises

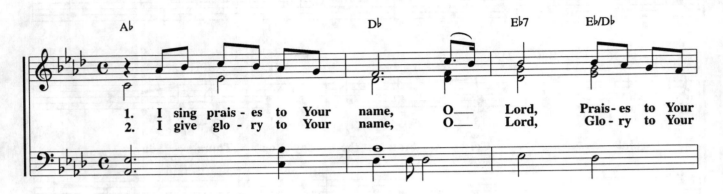

Words and Music by
TERRY MAC ALMON
Arr. by Larry Haron

1. I sing prais-es to Your name, O— Lord, Prais-es to Your
2. I give glo-ry to Your name, O— Lord, Glo-ry to Your

name, O— Lord, for Your name is great and
name, O— Lord, for Your name is great and

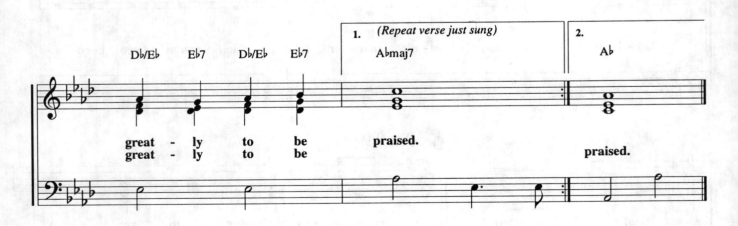

1. *(Repeat verse just sung)*
great - ly to be praised.
great - ly to be praised.

2.
praised.

Love Him in the Morning
(All Day Song)

107

Words and Music by
JOHN FISCHER
Arr. by Larry Haron

Love Him in the morn - in' when you see the sun a - ris - in',

Love Him in the eve - nin' 'cause He took you through the day;

And in the in - be - tween times when you feel the pres - sure com - in',

Re - mem - ber that He loves you and He prom - is - es to stay.

108   Seek Ye First

Based on Matthew 6:33; 7:7

Words and Music by
KAREN LAFFERTY
Arr. by Larry Haron

1. Seek ye first the kingdom of God, And His righteousness, And all these things shall be added unto you. Alleleu, Allelu - ia!
2. Ask and it shall be given unto you, Seek and ye shall find, Knock and the door shall be opened unto you. Allelu, Allelu - ia!

My Jesus, I Love Thee

109

WILLIAM R. FEATHERSTON

ADONIRAM J. GORDON
Arr. by Larry Haron

1. My Je - sus, I love Thee, I know Thou art mine. For
2. I love Thee be - cause Thou hast first lov - ed me And
3. In man - sions of glo - ry and end - less de - light, I'll

Thee all the fol - lies of sin I re - sign; My
pur - chased my par - don on Cal - va - ry's tree; I
ev - er a - dore Thee in heav - en so bright; I'll

gra - cious Re - deem - er, my Sav - ior art Thou: If
love Thee for wear - ing the thorns on Thy brow: If
sing with the glit - ter - ing crown on my brow: "If

ev - er I loved Thee, My Je - sus, 'tis now.
ev - er I loved Thee, My Je - sus, 'tis now.
ev - er I loved Thee, My Je - sus, 'tis now."

110

I Exalt Thee

Words and Music by
PETE SANCHEZ, JR.
Arr. by Larry Haron

My Country, 'Tis of Thee

111

SAMUEL F. SMITH

THESAURUS MUSICUS, c. 1745
Arr. by Larry Haron

112 I Am Thankful to Be an American

Words and Music by
OTIS SKILLINGS
Arr. by Larry Haron

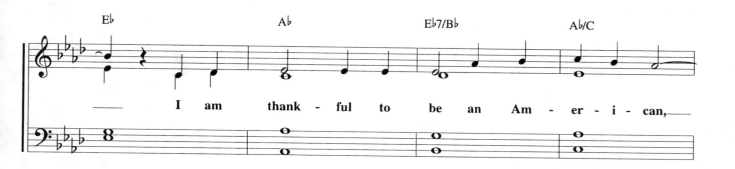

I am thank - ful to be an Am - er - i - can,

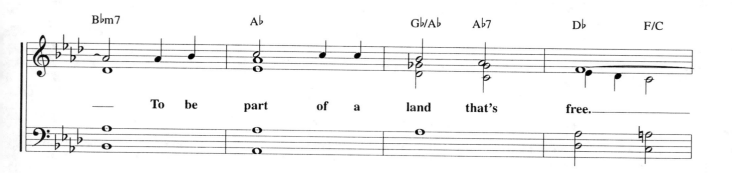

To be part of a land that's free.

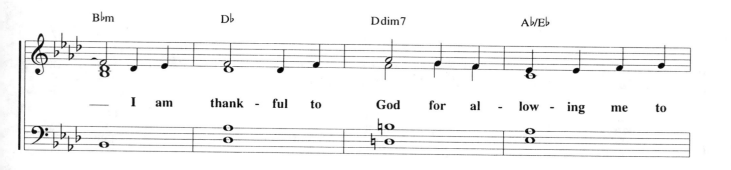

I am thank - ful to God for al - low - ing me to

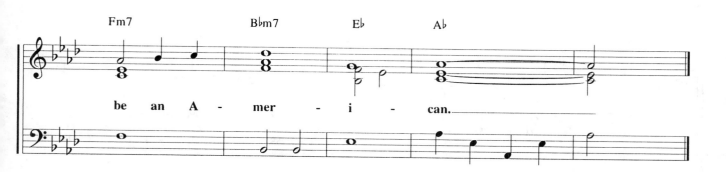

be an A - mer - i - can.

113 America, the Beautiful

KATHARINE LEE BATES

SAMUEL A. WARD
Arr. by Larry Haron

1. O beau - ti - ful for spa - cious skies, For am - ber waves of grain, For pur - ple moun - tain maj - es - ties A - bove the fruit - ed plain! A - mer - i - ca! A - mer - i - ca! God shed His grace on thee, And crown thy good with broth - er - hood From sea to shin - ing sea!
2. O beau - ti - ful for pil - grim feet, Whose stern im - pas - sioned stress A thor - ough - fare for free - dom beat A - cross the wil - der - ness! A - mer - i - ca! A - mer - i - ca! God mend thine ev - ery flaw, Con - firm thy soul in self - con - trol, Thy lib - er - ty in law!
3. O beau - ti - ful for he - roes proved In lib - er - at - ing strife, Who more than self their coun - try loved, And mer - cy more than life! A - mer - i - ca! A - mer - i - ca! May God thy gold re - fine, Till all suc - cess be no - ble - ness, And ev - ery gain di - vine!
4. O beau - ti - ful for pa - triot dream That sees be - yond the years Thine al - a - bas - ter cit - ies gleam, Un - dimmed by hu - man tears! A - mer - i - ca! A - mer - i - ca! God shed His grace on thee, And crown thy good with broth - er - hood From sea to shin - ing sea!

Say to the Lord, "I Love You" 114

Words and Music by
ERNIE RETTINO and DEBBIE KERNER RETTINO
Arr. by Larry Haron

115 Our God Reigns

Words and Music by
LEONARD E. SMITH, JR.
Arr. by Larry Haron

1. How love-ly on the moun-tains are the feet of him
2. He had no state-ly form, He had no maj-es-ty,
3. Out from the tomb He came with grace and maj-es-ty,

who brings good news, good news An-nounc-ing
That we should be drawn to Him. He was de-
He is a-live, He is a-live. God loves us

peace, pro-claim-ing news of hap-pi-ness. Yet Our God
spised and we took no ac-count of Him, now He
so, see here His hands, His feet, His side. Yes, we

reigns, Our God reigns!
reigns with the Most High. } Our God reigns!
know, He is a-live.

Our God reigns!____ Our God reigns!____ Our God reigns!

I Love You, Lord

116

Words and Music by
LAURIE KLEIN
Arr. by Larry Haron

I love You, Lord,____ and I lift my voice____ to

wor - ship You. O my soul, re - joice! Take joy, my King,____ in

what You hear:____ may it be a sweet, sweet____ sound in__ Your ear.____

117 In Moments Like These

Words and Music by
DAVID GRAHAM
Arr. by Larry Haron

In mo-ments like these I sing out a song, I sing out a love song to Je-sus. In mo-ments like these I lift up my hands, *(heart,)* I lift up my hands to the *(heart)* Lord._____ Sing-ing I love You, Lord,_____ sing-ing I love You, Lord,_____ sing-ing I love You, Lord,_____ I love You._____

Crown Him with Many Crowns   118

MATTHEW BRIDGES, stanzas 1, 2, 4
GODFREY THRING, stanza 3

GEORGE J. ELVEY
Arr. by Larry Haron

119 Great Is Thy Faithfulness

THOMAS O. CHISHOLM

WILLIAM M. RUNYAN
Arr. by Larry Haron

1. Great is Thy faith-ful-ness, O God my Fa-ther,
2. Sum-mer and win-ter, and spring-time and har-vest,
3. Par-don for sin and a peace that en-dur-eth,

There is no shad-ow of turn-ing with Thee;
Sun, moon and stars in their cours-es a-bove
Thy own dear pres-ence to cheer and to guide;

Thou chang-est not, Thy com-pas-sions they fail not;
Join with all na-ture in man-i-fold wit-ness
Strength for to-day and bright hope for to-mor-row,

As Thou hast been Thou for-ev-er wilt be.
To Thy great faith-ful-ness, mer-cy and love.
Bless-ings all mine, with ten thou-sand be-side!

120   Shout Hosanna

Words and Music by
ROBERT C. EVANS
Arr. by Larry Haron

1. Jump-ing up and down, jump-ing up and down,
2. Je-sus is a-live, Je-sus is a-live,

jump-ing up and down, shout, "Ho - san - na. Ho - san-na!"
Je-sus is a-live, shout, "Ho - san - na. Ho - san-na!"

Here comes Je-sus, rid-ing on a don-key, ho-
Here comes Je-sus, ris-ing up in glo-ry, ho-

san - na,——— ho - san-na, ho - san - na to the King.
san - na,——— ho - san-na, ho - san - na to the King.

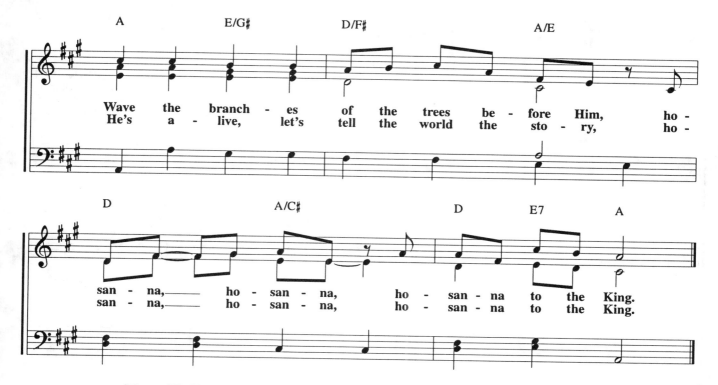

Wave the branch - es of the trees be - fore Him, ho -
He's a - live, let's of tell the world the sto - ry, ho -

san - na,_____ ho - san - na, ho - san - na to the King.
san - na,_____ ho - san - na, ho - san - na to the King.

In My Life, Lord, Be Glorified 121

Words and Music by
BOB KILPATRICK
Arr. by Larry Haron

1. In my life, Lord, be glo - ri - fied, be glo - ri - fied,
2. In my song, Lord, be glo - ri - fied, be glo - ri - fied,
3. In Your Church, Lord, be glo - ri - fied, be glo - ri - fied,

In my life, Lord, be glo - ri - fied to - day.
In my song, Lord, be glo - ri - fied to - day.
In Your Church, Lord, be glo - ri - fied to - day.

122 What a Mighty God We Serve

UNKNOWN
Arr. by Larry Haron

Cast Your Burden

TRADITIONAL
Arr. by Larry Haron

124 Sweet Song of Salvation

Words and Music by
LARRY NORMAN
Arr. by Larry Haron

Sing __ that sweet song of sal-va - tion, and let your laugh-ter fill __ the air.

__ Sing that sweet song of sal - va - tion __ and tell the

peo - ple ev - 'ry - where. Sing that __ sweet song of sal-va-

- tion __ to ev - 'ry man and ev-er-y na - tion, __ sing that

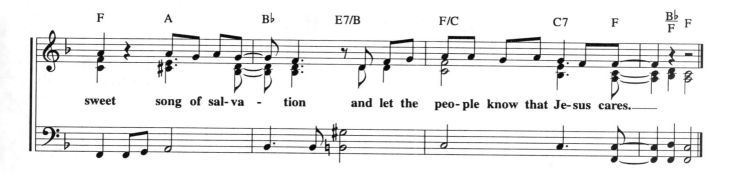

sweet song of sal-va - tion and let the peo-ple know that Je-sus cares.

O, How I Love Jesus

125

FREDERICK WHITFIELD

TRADITIONAL AMERICAN MELODY
Arr. by Larry Haron

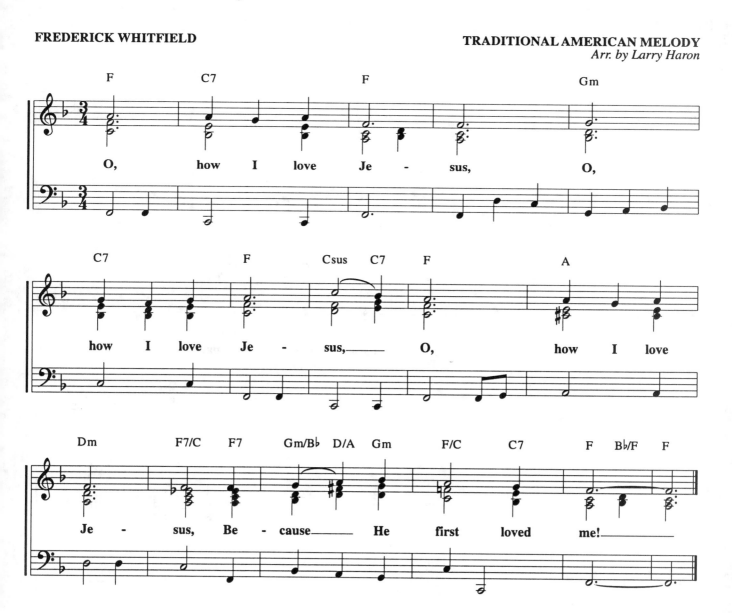

O, how I love Je - sus, O,

how I love Je - sus,_____ O, how I love

Je - sus, Be - cause_____ He first loved me!_____

126   I Will Bless the Lord

Words and Music by
FRANK HERNANDEZ
Arr. by Larry Haron

Jesus Is Lord of All

127

Words and Music by
ERNIE RETTINO and DEBBY KERNER RETTINO
Arr. by Larry Haron

128 No Way! We Are Not Ashamed

Words and Music by
CARMAN
Arr. by Larry Haron

No way, we are not a-shamed of the gos-pel or His name. Ho-ly hands *(hearts)* are lift-ed high to the name of Je-sus Christ.

1. Je-sus Christ.

129 This Is the Day

PSALM 118:24

LES GARRETT
Arr. by Larry Haron

This is the day, this is the day that the Lord has made, that the

130   The Countdown Song

Words and Music by
DOROTHY MONTGOMERY
Arr. by Larry Haron

Some-where in out-er space, God has pre-pared a place

For those who trust Him and o - bey.

Je - sus will come a - gain, Al - though we don't know when, The

count - down's get - ting low - er ev - ery day.

131 I Will Call upon the Lord

Words and Music by
MICHAEL O'SHIELDS

132 Make Your Dad Glad

Words and Music by
ROBERT C. EVANS

○ Blow kisses
△ Put arms around each other's
shoulders, imitating a barbershop quartet

▭ Tickle person next to you
▭ Cup hands around mouth

The Amazin' Praise 'n' Worship Quiz
Musical #1

Synopsis

Welcome to **The Amazin' Praise 'n' Worship Quiz.** Your host, P.W. Singer, and his assistant, Little David, lead you through songs, questions, and crazy stunts that will have you laughing and learning about the amazing world of praising.

Song Titles

Opening .... We're Singing Praises
Scene One .... Amen, Praise the Lord
Scene Two .... I Will Sing of the Mercies
Scene Three .... O for a Thousand Tongues
Scene Four .... Clap Your Hands
Scene Five .... Rejoice in the Lord Always
Scene Six .... My God Is So Great, So Strong and So Mighty
Scene Seven .... To God Be the Glory

Cast and Set

P.W. Singer .... The Quiz game show host and clown. He has an animated voice (sort of like Roger Rabbit) and over-exaggerates everything. He maintains a fast pace. Should be played by a teenager or adult in costume.

Little David .... P.W.'s silent assistant. A boy or small, older teenage boy. His job is to hold up cues for the audience and lead/direct their response. Note: last scene, little David appears bandaged up like an accident victim, one arm in a sling.

Contestants .... Betty Lou Blue, Chris Clark, Lindsay Little, and Randy Redding.

Props:
Honking Horn for Little David
Desk bell for Little David
Little David's 7 cue cards: "APPLAUSE"; "WITH MY MOUTH"; "TONGUES"; "CLAP YOUR HANDS"; "NO"; "ALWAYS"; "BYE, BYE".
Bowl of crackers
Small table with water glass and grape
Fake barbells, with "10,000 lbs" written on them

Script

Opening

[Choir: WE'RE SINGING PRAISES]

Scene One

Following song, kids sit down. Little David enters and holds up APPLAUSE sign. P.W. enters to applause.

P.W.: **Well, hello kids, and welcome to The Amazin' Praise 'n' Worship Quiz, where we have lots of fun learning about the amazin' world of praisin'! I'm your host, P.W. Singer!**

(For the rest of the show, Little David will cue the kids to cheer, answer questions, countdown, etc. Kids will respond accordingly. David's sign is indicated in All Caps)

APPLAUSE; kids cheer.

P.W.: **And please welcome my amazin' assistant, Little David!**

Kids cheer; David takes a bow.

P.W.: **Little David is also a talented songwriter, plays the harp, and swings a mean slingshot . . . .**

Kids "ooh"; Little David smiles.

P.W.: **. . . but today, he'll be helping us discover how to praise the Lord! Are you kids ready?**

APPLAUSE; kids cheer. Cue music.

P.W.: **Okay, let's get started by <u>singing</u>!**

[Choir: AMEN, PRAISE THE LORD]

During songs, kids stand and sing to audience, doing motions if called for. P.W. dances around to one side, enjoying the music; Little David remains in place, watching. When the song is over, kids return to be seated and P.W. returns center.

Scene Two

APPLAUSE; kids cheer.

P.W.: **Okay, kids, it's time for the first contestant in The Amazin' Praise 'n' Worship Quiz! Do I have a volunteer?**

Kids raise their hands, excited.

P.W.: **Betty Lou Blue, come up here and <u>amaze us</u>!**

APPLAUSE; kids cheer. Betty Lou comes forward.

P.W.: **Betty Lou, I'm going to ask you a question, and you'll have ten seconds to answer. If you fail to answer correctly, then we have a Praisin' Amazin' Activity for you - and <u>wait 'til you see what it is!</u> Are you ready? Listen carefully. Here is your question: Psalm 89:1 says, "I will sing of the mercies of the Lord forever. With my (blank) I will make known Thy faithfulness." What word goes in that blank? You have ten seconds. Go!**

Betty Lou thinks. As each contestant thinks of the answer, Little David will hold up his fingers and lead some of the children in the ten-second countdown (Ten, nine, eight . . .). Other kids will cheer for the contestant or shout answers at them.

P.W.: **Time's up! Betty Lou, can you tell us the answer? With my <u>what</u> will I make known God's faithfulness?**

Betty: **With my . . . voice?**

Little David honks the horn; kids sigh.

P.W.: **No, but that's close. Kids, what is the correct answer?**

David holds up card and kids shout WITH MY <u>MOUTH</u>.

P.W.: **That's right. "with my <u>mouth</u>." Now, Betty Lou, we don't want you to forget that, so we have a Praisin' Amazin' Activity to help you remember! Are you ready?**

Kids cheer. David brings out bowl of crackers.

P.W.: **Betty Lou, I have here a bowl of crackers. We want to see <u>how many</u> you can stuff in your mouth in ten seconds.** (Kids laugh.) **Are you ready? Go!**

David leads ten second countdown. Some kids cheer Betty Lou on as she stuffs crackers in her mouth. (NOTE TO DIRECTOR: As a safety precaution against choking, please be sure Betty Lou is not actually stuffing the crackers in her mouth, but is only "appearing" to!)

P.W.:   **Time's up! Great job, Betty Lou!**

APPLAUSE; kids cheer. Betty Lou nods, her mouth appearing to be full.

P.W.:   **Now, Betty Lou, with <u>what</u> do I make known God's faithfulness?**

Betty: (muffled) **Wth mm-mth.**

APPLAUSE; kids cheer. David rings bell.

P.W.:   **That's right! Let's give Betty Lou a hand!**

APPLAUSE; kids cheer. Cue music. Betty Lou exits with crackers.

[Choir: I WILL SING OF THE MERCIES]

Scene Three

P.W.:   **Okay, who'd like to be our next contestant?**

Kids respond.

P.W.:   **Chris Clark, come up here and <u>amaze us!</u>**

APPLAUSE; kids cheer as Chris comes up.

P.W.:   **Chris, here's your Amazin' Praise 'n' Worship Quiz question: A famous hymn says, "O for a thousand (blank) to sing." What is the correct answer? You have ten seconds! Go!**

David leads countdown. Kids cheer Chris on and shout answers at him.

P.W.:   **Time's up! Chris, "O for a thousand <u>whats</u> to sing?"**

Chris: **Mouths?**

Kids sigh; David honks the horn.

P.W.:   **No, I'm sorry. What's the answer, kids?**

David holds up cue card and kids shout "TONGUES!"

P.W.:   **Shall we show Chris his Praisin' Amazin' Activity?**

APPLAUSE; kids cheer. David brings out a table with water glass and a grape on it. P.W. takes Chris and the grape to the other side of the stage from the table.

P.W.: **Okay, Chris. Stick out your tongue!**

Kids laugh. Chris sticks out his tongue.

P.W.: **You're going to carry this grape on your tongue across to that table and drop it in the water glass, <u>without using your hands!</u>**

Kids laugh.

P.W.: **Oh boy! Are you ready? Go!**

David leads ten second countdown. Chris begins, drops grape, and starts again, making it to the glass and dropping the grape in. APPLAUSE; kids cheer.

P.W.: **Way to go, Chris! Let's all say the title of that hymn together.**

All: **"O for a Thousand Tongues to Sing"**

Cue music.

P.W.: **Let's hear it for Chris!**

APPLAUSE; kids cheer. Chris exits with table, glass and grape.

[Choir: O FOR A THOUSAND TONGUES]

Scene Four

P.W.: **You know, kids, there's something we've been doing on Amazin' Praise 'n' Worship Quiz that's a great way to praise God. Can you tell me what it is?**

David holds up cue card and kids shout "CLAP YOUR HANDS."

P.W.: **That's right! The Bible says, "Clap your hands, all ye people." Let's hear you clap your hands to praise God right now!**

APPLAUSE; kids cheer. Cue music.

P.W.: **That's be-autiful! Praise the Lord!**

[Choir: CLAP YOUR HANDS]

Scene Five

P.W.: **It's time for another contestant!**

Kids respond.

P.W.: **Lindsay Little, come up here and <u>amaze us!</u>**

APPLAUSE; kids cheer as Lindsay comes forward.

P.W.: **Lindsay, are you ready? Complete this poem:**

>   **We like to praise God
>   in both big and small ways.
>   Philippians tells us,
>   "Rejoice in Him – "**

Lindsay: (interrupting) **Always!**

APPLAUSE; kids cheer. David rings bell.

P.W.: **Wow, Lindsay! You didn't even need ten seconds to think about it! Isn't Lindsay amazin'!**

APPLAUSE; kids cheer

P.W.: **Kids, should we praise the Lord just on Sundays?**

David holds up cue card and kids shout, "NO"! David honks.

P.W.: **Oh, well – how about just on Mondays?**

David holds up cue card and kids shout, "NO"! David honks.

P.W.: **How about just when we feel like it?**

David holds up cue card and kids shout, "NO"! David honks.

P.W.: **When <u>should</u> we rejoice?**

David holds up cue card and kids shout, "ALWAYS"! David rings bell. Cue music.

[Choir: REJOICE IN THE LORD ALWAYS]

Scene Six

P.W.:   **It's time for our last contestant on Amazin' Praise 'n' Worship Quiz, and I hope they get this answer right, 'cause you won't believe what the Praisin' Amazin' Activity is if they don't. Now, who's it gonna be?**

Kids respond.

P.W.:   **Randy Redding, come up here and <u>amaze us!</u>**

APPLAUSE; kids cheer as Randy comes up.

P.W.:   **Randy, this is our last question for today. Are you ready? Complete this poem:**

> **Our God is so great**
> **We sing Him this song**
> **We praise Him because**
> **He is mighty and (blank).**

Randy, what is the correct word to complete the poem? You have ten seconds. Go!

David leads ten second countdown. Some kids cheer for Randy and shout answers.

P.W.:   **It's time for our final answer. Randy,**

> **Our God is so great**
> **We sing Him this song**
> **We praise Him because**
> **He is mighty and . . . .**

Randy: **Strong?**

Kids gasp, waiting.

P.W.:   **Randy . . . you . . . are . . .**

Kids gasp again.

P.W.:   **ABSOLUTELY RIGHT!**

APPLAUSE; kid cheer. David rings the bell.

P.W.:   **Yes! Our God is so great, so strong, and so mighty. That's another reason we praise Him. And boy, you'd better be glad you knew the answer, because otherwise you'd have had to lift this <u>ten thousand pound weight!</u> Little David, <u>show him the weight!</u>**

Kids cheer as Little David struggles across the stage with the barbells, losing his balance and finally crashing offstage. Kids laugh.

P.W.: **Uh-oh. Looks like we'd better sing a song while I go check on David. Everybody <u>sing</u>!**

Kids cheer as P.W. exits to see about David.

[Choir: MY GOD IS SO GREAT, SO STRONG AND SO MIGHTY]

Scene Seven

P.W. has returned. David has also returned, all bandaged up like an accident victim, one arm in a sling. He stands center with P.W.

P.W.: **Well, kids, that's about all for today. My assistant, Little David, and I would like to thank you for joining us!**

Kids cheer; David bows painfully.

P.W.: **And you know, we've done some crazy things here today, but I hope you've learned how important it is to praise God. He loves to hear us sing, and since He is such a great God, we have a lot to sing about! So let's sing one more song before we go, and until our next show, remember . . . praisin' is amazin'!**

Cue music; kids cheer. P.W. waves and David holds up cue card reading BYE, BYE with his one good hand.

[Choir: TO GOD BE THE GLORY]

THE END

PARENT'S NIGHT
Musical #2

Synopsis

Mrs. Lunn is rehearsing the Vacation Bible School classes for their Parent's Night program. Through the scenes in the program, the children tell the Bible stories they have been learning in VBS all week. All is not going according to Mrs. Lunn's plans! Will the program be ready for Parent's Night? Join us for a not-quite-perfect dress rehearsal.

Song Titles

Opening .... The B-I-B-L-E
Scene One .... Father Abraham
Scene Two .... Arky, Arky
Scene Three .... How Did Moses Cross the Red Sea
Scene Four .... Ten Commandments Song
Scene Five .... Only a Boy Named David
Scene Six .... Zaccheus
Scene Seven .... Give Thanks
Scene Eight .... Thy Word

Cast

Mrs. Lunn	The VBS Director; may be an adult of any age. Dressed in a casual skirt and summer blouse. Carries a clipboard and pencil; wears a watch.
Jeffrey	Boy
Narrator 1–7	Boy or girl; these characters will stand at podium and read the story from pages they carry; therefore, they will not need to memorize the part.
Child 1-7	Boy or girl; these characters will carry the placards and announce each scene; Child 5 and 6 also speak a few additional lines.
Class Member 1–10	Boy or girl; these children each have one line, reciting one of the Ten Commandments; younger children will be good candidates for these simple parts.
David	Boy; has major lines in Scene Five.

Set, Props and Costumes

Set

Stage may be left bare, cleared of pulpit and furniture. Scenes are played centerstage. Entrances and exits marked stage left and right may be done by coming up steps or by entering from the choir loft doors.

Extra set pieces and props can just be leaned against the back of stage, creating an unorganized, rehearsal look. These can be carried in by the children during the opening, or may already be in place at the beginning.

Props

Scene 1
- Placard reading "Father of Many Nations"
- Narrator 1's script
- Abraham's "tent": a large appliance-size cardboard box, with a door cut out and a cloth or rug thrown over the roof
- Cotton rug, wooden bowls for Abraham's tent
- Sarah's broom
- Baby doll, wrapped in cloth
- Similar dolls for other "women"

Scene 2
- Placard reading "The Ark, the Flood and the Rainbow"
- Narrator 2's script
- Ark: cut from the side of a large cardboard box and painted, with windows cut out. Must be large enough for children to stand behind and look through.
- Bedrolls, baskets, pots for relatives to carry as their belongings
- Rainbow Banner: white butcher paper, with a rainbow painted across it, and the words "The End" in center.

Scene 3
- Placard reading "Moses Parts the Red Sea"
- Narrator 3's script
- Red Sea: Two sections of white butcher paper, painted with waves of water. Each is carried by two children. At first, they are carried together as one "sea." Later, they part.
- Bedrolls, baskets, pots, etc. (used in Scene 2 above), which the children of Israel carry as their belongings.
- Swords, cut out of cardboard, for the Egyptians

Scene 4
- Narrator 4's script
- Ten Commandment tablets: Two large tablets, cut from styrofoam or heavy cardboard, and painted to look like chiseled stone. One should then be bent, and one torn

part way down the center, as if they were in an accident.

Scene 5   •   Placard reading "David and the Giant"

Scene 7   •   Placard reading "The Man Who Said 'Thank You'"
             •   Narrator 7's script

Costumes

Choir   Dressed in summer playwear; what you would wear to VBS

Choir members used as extras to play townspeople, family members, children of Israel, etc. should wear simple costumes over their street clothes:

- Boys: wear bathrobes; use dishtowels wrapped around as headdresses.
- Boys who are Egyptians may wear helmets brought from home, rather than headdresses.
- Girls should wear a twin sheet, wrapped around them and tied like a sarong, and a dishtowel as a headdress.

Abraham, Noah, and Moses may wear beards.

Ark Animals   These may be represented by paper masks, painted and decorated to resemble the animals listed in Scene 2. Tails, feathers, fins, scales, or a trunk may be attached to street clothes for added touches.

Cloud   Make a sandwich board of two large cardboard pieces cut in cloud shape and painted white. The child should wear white clothes, and may also wear a white baseball cap with cotton attached all over it.

David   David's "armor" can be cut from sheets of poster board: a breastplate, arm pieces, and two shin guards. See diagram below.

The "helmet" can be cut from a grocery bag. See diagram below.

Jesus   Jesus' robes may be made by cutting a hole in the center of a white double top sheet for his head. Drape the sheet over him, letting his arms stick out the sides, and tie a rope for a belt, blousing the sheet to resemble a robe. Jesus should also wear a beard (see note above for Abraham, etc.)

Lepers   Tear white sheets in long strips and wrap lepers, mummy style. When they are healed, they can unwrap their hands and feet to examine them.

Script

OPENING
[Choir: THE B-I-B-L-E]

SCENE ONE
Father of Many Nations

Kids are milling around, talking, some kids are carrying in more set pieces and props. Mrs. Lunn enters, carrying a clipboard and pencil. She is obviously very hurried.

Mrs. Lunn: **Children! Children! It's time for dress rehearsal. Let's all sit down at the front of the stage. Everybody! Come on! Sit, sit, sit!**

Kids gather around her at front center and sit on the floor.

Mrs. Lunn: **As you all know, Parent's Night is tonight, and I hope you have all invited your parents to see our Vacation Bible School pageant. We want them to see all the wonderful Bible stories we have been learning this week.** (A child raises his hand.) **Uh . . yes, Jeffrey?**

Jeffrey: **My mom's out of town; she's at my grandmother's.**

Mrs. Lunn: (trying to get on with it) **Well, I'm sorry about that.**

Jeffrey: **My dad's bringing me by himself.**

Mrs. Lunn: **Well, isn't that nice.**

Jeffrey: **He said he hopes this isn't too long. There's a baseball game at 9:00.**

Mrs. Lunn: **We'll try to get out in plenty of time.** (rushing on) **Now, children, we're going to run through each class's scene. Then everyone will sing the songs. Tonight, you'll be backstage during the scenes . . . but for now, you can just sit to the sides and watch.** (They start to get up and move aside.) **But BE QUIET!** (They move aside, and she calls the first group.) **Okay, Mrs. Hart's class . . . you have Scene One.**

Teacher moves her group into place. Narrator comes to mic, and prepares to read. One child comes to center with the placard which reads "Father of Many Nations," and introduces the scene.

Child 1: (shouting) **Mrs. Hart's class presents "Abraham: Father of Many Nations."**

Child 1 moves aside, puts the placard against the back of the stage, and rejoins the group. Abraham comes to center.

Narrator 1: (reading) **There was a man named Abraham, who was ninety-nine years old. And God appeared to him and said, "I have a promise for you."**

(Abraham looks up and out, as if he hears God speak to him.)

Narrator 1: **And Abraham fell on his face before God.**

(Abraham falls to his knees, and bows down to the ground.)

Narrator 1: **And God said to Abraham, "Behold, I will make you the father of many nations. And if you keep my commandments, your children will inherit the Promised Land." And Abraham laughed.**

(Abraham sits up and laughs.)

Narrator 1: **He said, "How can an old man have a child?" But God said, "I will do it."**

Abraham gets up and helps Sarah to move in his tent. He sits down in front of it.

Narrator 1: **One day, Abraham was sitting at the door to his tent, when three men came by.**

(Three men enter and cross to Abraham. He gets up and shakes their hands.)

Narrator 1: **Abraham invited them to stay for dinner.**

(Abraham indicates for the men to sit. Sarah enters, and sets bowls in front of them on the ground. They pretend to eat. Sarah gets a broom and sweeps at one side of the tent, and eavesdrops.)

Narrator 1: **One of the men said, "Where is your wife, Sarah?" "In the tent," said Abraham.**

(The actors pantomime the following)

Narrator 1: **"Next year, at this time, she will have a son," said the visitor. Sarah laughed and laughed. "I am too old to have a child!" she said.**

(Sarah laughs. The men look at her, surprised. Embarassed, she exits.)

Narrator 1: **"Why did Sarah laugh?" said God. "Nothing is too hard for God." And a year later Sarah and Abraham had a son, even though they were very old.**

(The men exit, Sarah enters, carrying a baby; she and Abraham come to stand in the center, admiring their baby.)

Narrator 1: **And they named the baby Isaac, which means "laughter."**

(All the others in the group come to stand around Sarah and Abraham, some carrying babies.)

Narrator 1: **And Isaac's grandchildren were the beginning of the twelve tribes of Israel. So Abraham became the father of many nations, because nothing is too hard for God.**

The children watching the scene applaud, and the children in the scene bow. Cue music. Everyone gets up, sings, and does the body motions.

[Choir: FATHER ABRAHAM]

SCENE TWO
The Ark, the Flood and the Rainbow

Mrs. Lunn enters, her clipboard under her arm, applauding.

Mrs. Lunn: **Excellent, children.** (marking a check on her clipboard) **That's all of Scene One. Next is Mrs. Wright's class, with Scene Two.**

Kids in Scene Two group jump up and teacher begins to direct them to their places. Several children get the set pieces needed and carry them offstage. Noah, Mrs. Noah, and their kids line up across the center. Child 2 comes center to stand in front of them, bearing a placard which reads "The Ark, the Flood, and the Rainbow."

Child 2: (very loudly and overdramatically) **Mrs. Wright's class presents "The Ark, the Flood, and the Rainbow."**

Everyone laughs because the child is so overly dramatic. Child 2 looks questioningly at the teacher, who kindly gives the child an "OK" sign; Child 2 exits, reassured.

Narrator 2: **There once was a man named Noah. God told Noah he was very unhappy with the way people were acting. "No one obeys me anymore," God said. "I am going to send a flood to destroy everyone." God told Noah to build a huge ship, called an ark.**

Several kids carry out the ark, and hold it, stage left.

Narrator 2: **People laughed at Noah for building such a big boat, when there was no water around for miles.**

Townspeople stage left laugh and point at Noah and the ark, making fun.

Narrator 2: **But Noah trusted God.**

Townspeople exit.

Narrator 2: **Then God told Noah to put two of every kind of animal on the ark.**

Noah crosses to stage right and motions for animals to enter and follow him. Animals enter in pairs, following Noah to the ark, where they "enter" by walking behind it and disappearing offstage left. Noah stands by the ark and herds the animals on.

Narrator 2: **Noah made sure there were two of everything. There were tigers, cows, dogs, cats, elephants, zebras, . . . even birds and bugs.**

The Narrator says each animal as they enter.

Narrator 2: **Then Noah put his family on the ark . . .**

Noah goes to his family, and brings them to the ark, where they "enter." Instead of exiting offstage, they remain behind the ark, looking out. A few animals may come back and join them, for effect.

Narrator 2: **. . . All his family, even the cousins.**

Noah goes back to get the cousins, aunts, uncles, etc. who enter stage right. They "enter" the ark also, but exit the stage.

Narrator 2: **Then God said, "It's time. Get on the ark." So Noah got on the ark, and God closed the door behind him.**

Noah "enters" the ark and remains with his family, looking out.

Narrator 2: **Then God sent the floods.**

The "ark" begins to slowly shuffle across the stage toward stage left, rocking side to side. Its "passengers" move with it, bobbing up and down. During the next few lines, it moves back toward stage left and comes to rest in its original place.

Narrator 2: **For forty days and nights, it rained. It rained HARD.**

Narrator 2: **And the waters covered the earth, destroying everything. But Noah, his family and the animals were safe on the boat.**

One of the animals says "Moo-oo".

Narrator 2: **Then the rains stopped and the water dried up.**

The ark stops moving, and the passengers say "A-a-h-h-" with relief.

Narrator 2: **And Noah and his family came out of the ark with all the animals, onto dry ground.**

All the people and animals who originally boarded the ark now reenter the stage, as if coming off the ark.

Narrator 2:   **Then God sent a rainbow in the sky as a promise that He would never destroy the earth with a flood again.**

Two kids enter with the rainbow banner. The kids watching applaud and cheer. All the kids onstage, including animals, ark, rainbow, etc. take a bow. Cue music.

[Choir: ARKY, ARKY]

SCENE THREE
Moses Parts the Red Sea

Following the song, the kids begin to clear the stage, going back to their places. Mrs. Lunn enters, clapping and calls over the top of their noise.

Mrs. Lunn: **Let's try Scene Three . . . Miss McLemore's class on stage!**

Teacher gets class together and positions them on stage left. Moses stands in front of them, as leader. Child 3 comes to center front with placard reading "Moses Parts the Red Sea," and introduces the scene. Child 3 begins too nervously and softly.

Child 3:   (nervously and softly) **Mosses-s Parts-s the Red . . .**

Mrs. Lunn: **Speak up! Project!**

Child 3:   (shouting) **Miss McLemore's class presents "Moses Parts the Red Sea!"**

Everyone laughs. Child 3 exits.

Mrs. Lunn: **Much better!**

Narrator 3:   (reads, hesitating over hard words) **Now, Moses and the children of Is . . Is . .**

One of the children of Israel whispers loudly, "Israel!"

Narrator 3:   **. . Israel had been in ex . . ex . .**

Narrator 3 stops, frustrated. All the children of Israel sigh loudly, irritated.

Narrator 3:   (brightening) **I got it! Exile! Now, Moses and the children of Is . . Is . .**

One of the children of Israel says, loudly, "Here we go again!"

Mrs. Lunn: **Skip over that part, dear.**

Narrator 3:   **They wanted to get out of Egypt and go back to their home. So God sent plagues upon Egypt until finally Pharoah said they could leave.**

Moses: (motioning to the children of Israel) **Let's get out of here!**

The children of Israel begin to follow Moses across the stage.

Narrator 3: **Moses led them to the bank of the Red Sea, where they made camp.**

Kids holding the Red Sea enter and block the children of Israel's exit offstage right. The children of Israel put down their things and lay down to sleep.

Narrator 3: **But they didn't know Egyptians were chasing them, and when they saw them, the children of Israel were afraid.**

The Egyptians enter stage left and shake their swords at the children of Israel, who wake up, see them and begin to carry on in fear.

Narrator 3: **Moses said, "STOP!"** (Moses stands up and throws out his arms, pantomiming this.) **"Do not be afraid! God will do something wonderful for us!" Then God said to Moses, "What are you yelling about? Get up and go on."**

The children of Israel get up and get their belongings together.

Narrator 3: **Then God put a cloud between the Egyptians and Israel, so the Egyptians couldn't see what was going on.**

Cloud comes and stands between the two groups, holding out his arms to block the view. The Egyptians turn and look at each other, shrugging and scratching their heads like "What happened?"

Narrator 3: **Then Moses stretched out his hand, the Red Sea <u>parted</u>, and the children of Israel walked right through to the other side.**

The actors pantomime this, and the children of Israel pass through the Red Sea and exit the stage victoriously. The Cloud follows them. When it does, the Egyptians suddenly point to each other as if they can see what's going on. They head toward the Red Sea.

Narrator 3: **The Egyptians tried to follow them.**

Moses re-enters from stage right, with the Red Sea between him and the Egyptians, and stretches out his hand again.

Narrator 3: **But Moses stretched out his hand again, and the sea swallowed up all the Egyptians!**

The children carrying the Red Sea swirl all around the Egyptians, who fall down dead in a pile. The "Sea" sits on top of the pile.

Narrator 3:	**Then the children of Israel sang and praised the Lord!**

Moses and the children of Israel re-enter, dancing and jumping happily. The children watching applaud. Cue music.

[Choir: HOW DID MOSES CROSS THE RED SEA]

SCENE FOUR
The Ten Commandments

Mrs. Lunn enters, checking her clipboard.

Mrs. Lunn:	**Let's see . . . next scene . . . the Ten Commandments. Mrs. Davidson's class . . . line up!**

Mrs. Davidson's class lines up, ten to a row across the center. Narrator 4 comes to the podium. They stand in awkward silence for a moment. Obviously they are waiting for someone to do their part.

Mrs. Lunn:	**Narrator, begin!**
Narrator 4:	**Betsy's supposed to announce the scene first!**
Mrs. Lunn:	**Where is Betsy?**
Child 4:	**She's not here today; but she <u>will</u> be here tonight!**
Mrs. Lunn:	**Well, somebody get her sign and introduce this scene.**
Child 4:	(running off to get the sign) **I'll do it!**

There is a huge crash offstage.

Child 4:	**Uh - oh!**
Mrs. Lunn:	**What on earth happened back there?**

Child 4 re-enters, carrying the Ten Commandment tablets, which are torn up, and wearing a coat hanger on his head. All the children sigh, "Oh, no!"

Mrs. Lunn:	(shaking her head) **Well, it looks like we're going to need another set of tablets.**
Narrator 4:	**Actually, this is a lot like what happened in the Bible!**

All the children watching say "Huh?"

Narrator 4:	(looking through his pages of narration) **Yeah . . .** (reading) **Moses went up on the mountain, where God wrote the commandments on two tablets of stone. But when**

Moses came down, the children of Israel were disobeying God and worshiping a golden idol. Moses was angry, and he threw the tablets down and broke them.

Child 5: **So, how did they know the commandments?**

Narrator 4: **After the people had repented, God wrote them down again on two more tablets.**

Mrs. Lunn: **Well, we're going to have to write them down again, too. Fine . . . I'll get somebody to do that later. Children, just say your lines quickly and we'll move on.**

The children who are lined up across the stage each step forward and recite their commandment.

Class Member 1: **You shall have no other gods before me.**

Class Member 2: **You shall not worship idols.**

Class Member 3: **You shall not take the name of God in vain.**

Class Member 4: **Remember the Sabbath and keep it holy.**

Class Member 5: **Honor your Father and Mother.**

Class Member 6: **You shall not kill.**

Class Member 7: **You shall not commit adultery.**

Class Member 8: **You shall not steal.**

Class Member 9: **You shall not gossip or lie.**

Class Member 10: **You shall not covet what someone else has.**

All 10: **These are God's commandments.**

[Choir: TEN COMMANDMENTS SONG]

SCENE FIVE
David and the Giant

Mrs. Lunn: (looking at her watch) **We've got to speed things up here. We're running late. Miss Ward's class is next, with David and Goliath . . . are you ready?**

David enters, dressed in "armor," with Narrator 5, with papers in hand, and Child 5 with placard reading, "David and the Giant" following him.

David: **We're here, Mrs. Lunn. But Goliath had to go to the bathroom.**

Everyone laughs.

Mrs. Lunn: (distressed) **Well, we've just got to move on. We can't wait for Goliath.**

David: **Well, I can just <u>tell</u> you the story. I know how it goes.**

Mrs. Lunn: (thinking aloud, not paying attention to David) **I know we <u>do</u> need to rehearse this scene.**

David: **See, David is just this little kid, like me, but he's not afraid to fight the mean giant Goliath . . .**

Mrs. Lunn: **If we don't rehearse it now, there won't be time later, and it might not go well tonight in the performance.**

David: **The king gives him this big suit of armour, but David just takes his slingshot . . .**

Mrs. Lunn is unaware that the children have begun to pay close attention to David's story. She is still thinking aloud.

Mrs. Lunn: **If we wait on Goliath, we're going to be <u>further</u> behind!**

David: (becoming more dramatic) **Goliath <u>laughs</u> at this small boy. But David is not afraid. He knows that God is on his side. So he aims his slingshot . . .** (he pantomimes this)

Mrs. Lunn: **I think it would be better to go on, so we can get out on time. I know the children would like that.**

David: **. . . and WHAM! He gets the giant <u>right</u> between the eyes!**

The children applaud and cheer David's victory. Mrs. Lunn looks around, startled. She thinks they are applauding her decision.

Mrs. Lunn: **Yes! I'm glad you agree. Well, David, I'm sorry but you'll have to tell us your story another time. Now, what's next?**

She checks her clipboard and exits. David, Narrator 5, and Child 5 look at each other as if she's crazy, and shrug. Cue music.

[Choir: ONLY A BOY NAMED DAVID]

SCENE SIX
Zaccheus

Mrs. Lunn enters, pondering a problem. She pauses, looks around the stage, shakes her head, her hands on her hips.

Child 6:	**What's the matter, Mrs. Lunn?**
Mrs. Lunn:	**Well . . . Mrs. Woodley's class is supposed to present the story of Zaccheus now, but they've been having trouble figuring out how to get him up in a tree, so they don't think they can do the story.**
Kids:	**Oh.**
Mrs. Lunn:	**I guess we'll just have to leave out this scene.**
Kids:	**Oh, no!**
Child 6:	**Can't we still sing the song? It's my favorite.**

Kids ad lib, "Yeah . . . let us sing it . . . we love this one . . ." etc.

Mrs. Lunn:	(shrugging) **I guess so . . . Well, why not?**

Cue music. Kids cheer and jump up to sing.

[Choir: ZACCHEUS]

SCENE SEVEN
The Man Who Said "Thank You"

Mrs. Lunn:	**Now, let's see if we can manage to get the last scene rehearsed.** (checking her clipboard) **Mrs. Myer's class . . . are you all here, I hope?**

Mrs. Myer's class gets in place. Lepers gather at stage right in a group. Narrator 7 comes to podium.

Mrs. Lunn:	(looking about) **Characters? Narrator? Where's our introduction?**

Child 7 runs in with a placard which reads, "The Man Who Said 'Thank You.'"

Child 7:	**Here I am!**
Mrs. Lunn:	**Proceed.**
Child 7:	(breathless) **Mrs. Myer's class presents, "The Man Who Said 'Thank You.'"**
Narrator 7:	**One day Jesus was walking down the road with His disciples. They passed a group of lepers.**

Jesus and disciples enter stage left and move toward centerstage. The lepers come toward them. The disciples shrink back, not wanting to get near them.

Narrator 7: "Jesus! Help us!" cried the lepers. They knew Jesus could heal them.

The lepers pantomime pleading.

Narrator 7: Jesus said to them, "You are well. Go to the temple and show them."

The lepers examine themselves, amazed, and run off stage right. One leper stops.

Narrator 7: But one leper came back to Jesus. "Thank You!" he said to Jesus. "Thank You for making me well."

The leper runs to Jesus and falls at His feet, thanking Him.

Narrator 7: Jesus said to His disciples, "Look! Didn't I heal ten men? Only one has come back to thank Me. This man isn't even one of us. But he belongs to Me because he remembered to thank Me." He said to the man, "Your faith has made you well."

Cue music, Jesus motions for the man to rise and go, and he does, exiting, praising.

[Choir: GIVE THANKS]

SCENE EIGHT
The Finale

Mrs. Lunn: (touched by the last song, is wiping tears from her eyes) **Children, let's stop and pray.**

They all stop and bow their heads.

Mrs. Lunn: God, forgive me. I've been so busy, I almost forgot what this is all about. I almost forgot how great You are. Thank You for reminding me through these stories. Thank You for giving us the Bible, which helps us to know about You. We love You. Amen."

She opens her eyes and looks around, smiling. The children wait on her direction.

Mrs. Lunn: (happily) **Everyone on stage for the finale. Oh, children, I think this is going to be our best Parent's Night ever! Now let's see . . . I must remember to speak with Goliath about the scene he missed. Oh, and we need to make another set of Ten Commandment tablets . . . Oh, yes, this is going to be wonderful . . . Thank you, Lord!**

She exits, talking to herself. Cue music. All children come on stage for finale, in the costumes from each scene. Also, children carrying placards return with them. Some set pieces should be brought back in, like the arks, Red Sea, and Ten Commandment tablets.

[Choir: Finale - THY WORD]

THE END

SHOW AND TELL
Musical #3

Synopsis

Kelsey is excited because she just became a Christian, and she can't wait to get to school to tell her friends. But during "Show and Tell" time, Kelsey learns that it's not enough to tell people about the difference Christ makes in your heart; you also have to show them.

Song Titles

Opening .... Born Again
Scene One .... This Little Light of Mine
Scene Two .... Stop! and Let Me Tell You
Scene Three .... I Am a C-H-R-I-S-T-I-A-N
Scene Four .... Jesus Loves Me
Scene Five .... Into My Heart
Scene Six .... If You're Happy and You Know It
Scene Seven .... Blessed Assurance

Cast

Kelsey .... A third or fourth grade girl. She is very excited about becoming a Christian. Kelsey has trouble keeping her temper.

Lauren .... A fourth grade girl. Kelsey's best friend.

Mrs. Bowen .... Kelsey's teacher. May be any age woman.

Boy 1 .... Children in Kelsey's class.
Boy 2
Boy 3
Girl 1
Girl 2
Girl 3

Characters should be dressed for a typical school day. In Scenes One and Seven, Kelsey and the other girls will need jackets, book bags and lunch boxes.

Set and Props

Props ....1.   low chair for Mrs. Bowen

2.   small box with tooth for Brian

3.   various items brought by children for Show and Tell: stuffed animals, rocks, sticks, jars with liquid in them, etc.

Set ....1.   Scenes One and Seven can be played to one side of the stage, or on the steps leading up to stage. No set is needed.

2.   Scenes Two–Six may be set to the other side of the stage. Mrs. Bowen may enter and set her chair and the other children may carry in their props before the lights come up on the scene.

3.   Kelsey's "Dear Diary" sections can be prerecorded and played on cue during the performance. This allows the child playing Kelsey to read these lines rather than memorize them.

Script

OPENING
[Choir: BORN AGAIN]

SCENE ONE
Outside the School

VO Kelsey: **Dear Diary: Yesterday at church, the most wonderful thing happened to me – I became a Christian! In Sunday school, I prayed and asked Jesus to come into my heart. I couldn't wait to get to school today, so I could tell all my friends. Actually, I didn't think I'd have to tell them; they'd probably just take one look at me and see the difference. Well . . . that's not exactly what happened . . .**

Kelsey runs onstage. She stops, and turns to call back.

Kelsey: **Come on, Lauren, we'll be late for school!**

Lauren: (runs in, breathless) **Okay, I'm coming! What's the deal?**

Kelsey: **Today is Show and Tell. And I've got a great one!**

Lauren:	**What?**

Kelsey: **I'm going to tell them what happened to me yesterday at church. I'm going to tell them how I became a Christian!**

Lauren: (dubious) **That's great, Kelsey . . . but aren't you supposed to have something to <u>show</u> when you <u>tell</u>?**

Kelsey: **Yeah . . . me. They'll be able to see it by just looking at me. Can't you see that?**

Lauren: **I thought you were just sweaty from running to school.**

School bell rings.

Kelsey: **There's the bell! Come on, Lauren!** (She runs out.)

Lauren: **Okay, I'm coming.** (She exits.)

Cue music.

[Choir: THIS LITTLE LIGHT OF MINE]

SCENE TWO
The classroom

Class is seated in semicircle on the floor. Children have brought things for Show and Tell. Mrs. Bowen is seated in front of them on a low chair.

Mrs. Bowen: **Class, as you all know, this is our day for Show and Tell. I can see that you all have brought something to share. Who would like to go first?**

They all raise their hands, anxiously, ad libbing, "Me, me . . ."

Mrs. Bowen: **Brian?**

The others drop their hands, ad libbing, "Aw. . ." Brian stands up, delighted, and comes to the center to stand by Mrs. Bowen. He is holding a small box, like a department store jewelry gift box.

Mrs. Bowen: **What would you like to share with us, Brian?**

Brian: (with an obviously exaggerated lisp, sort of like Sylvester the Cat) **S-Something exc-c-iting that happened on S-Saturday!**

Everyone laughs.

Mrs. Bowen: **Goodness, Brian, you're talking funny this morning!**

Brian: (proudly) **Yes-s, ma'am.**

Mrs. Bowen: **Does that have something to do with your Show and Tell?**

Brian: **S-sure does-s!**

Everyone laughs again.

Mrs. Bowen: **Why don't you show us what's in the box.**

Removes the lid and holds out the box, showing it around the circle. Kids ad lib "W-o-w!" as they look in the box.

Brian: **It's-s my f-front tooth-th! It came out S-saturday!**

They applaud. He puts the lid back on the box and sits down.

Mrs. Bowen: **Very good, Brian! I think we can all agree that that was very s-special!** (She imitates Brian's exaggerated lisp, teasing him. Everyone laughs, including Brian.) **Now, who's next?**

The kids all raise their hands, ad libbing "Me, me . . ." They continue to pantomime as the scene fades and VO Kelsey begins.

VO Kelsey: **I thought she would <u>never</u> call on me. People had all <u>sorts</u> of weird things to show and tell. But nothing as important as mine. I thought I was going to have to shout, "Stop! You've just <u>got</u> to let me tell you about me!"**

[Choir: STOP! AND LET ME TELL YOU]

SCENE THREE
The Classroom

Kids have their hands raised, trying to get Mrs. Bowen's attention.

Kelsey: **Oh, please, Mrs. Bowen, you've got to call me next!**

Mrs. Bowen: **Kelsey, you look like you might pop if I don't! Okay, come on up.**

Other kids drop their hand, ad libbing, "Aw. . ." Kelsey comes to center.

Kelsey: **I'm going to tell you about something really exciting that happened to me this weekend, too!**

Boy 1:	**Well, where is it?**
Kelsey:	**Where is what?**
Boy 1:	**Your Show and Tell. Don't you have something to show?**
	Others ad lib, "Yeah . . . Where is it? . . . Show us!" etc.
Kelsey:	**Me! I'm it.**
Kids:	**You?**
Girl 1:	<u>**You're**</u> **the Show and Tell?**
	Others ad lib, "Aw . . ."
Boy 2:	**What's so special about you?**
Kelsey:	**It's what happened to me this weekend. Yesterday I became a C-H-R-I-S-T-I-A-N.**
Girl 2:	**A what?**
Kelsey:	(impatiently) **A C-H-R-I-S-T-I-A-N!**
Boy 2:	(slowly) **A C-H-R . . .**
Kelsey:	(losing her temper) **I'm a Christian, you dummy!**
	Cue music.
Boy 2:	**Oh . . . well, you don't have to shout.**

[Choir: I AM A C-H-R-I-S-T-I-A-N]

SCENE FOUR
The Classroom

The kids and Mrs. Bowen continue to pantomime as if Kelsey is talking to them and they are asking questions.

VO Kelsey:	**After they finally got it through their heads what a Christian was, Mrs. Bowen asked me to tell how it happened. So I told them the story my Sunday school teacher told us . . . how Jesus came to earth; how He loved people, especially the children, and how He died on the cross for our sin.**
Girl 3:	**That's a sad story.**

Kelsey:	It's sad, but it has a happy ending. He came back to life three days later . . . **because He was God.**
Boy 3:	If He was God, why did He die?
Kelsey:	To show us God's love. To tell us, "God loves you."
Boy 2:	I guess God likes Show and Tell, too!

Cue music.

[Choir: JESUS LOVES ME]

SCENE FIVE
The Classroom

Kelsey is still standing in the center of the group.

Girl 1:	You still haven't <u>told</u> us how you became a . . . a C-H-R-I- . . . I . . .
Kelsey:	(shouting) A Christian!
Girl 1:	(her feelings hurt) Right.
Kelsey:	(oblivious) After the story, our teacher said that if we loved Jesus, too, then we could pray and ask Him to live in our hearts. So I did.
Boy 1:	You did?
Boy 2:	Just like that?
	Kelsey nods.
Girl 3:	How?
Kelsey:	I just prayed. *I said "Jesus, I know You love me. And I love You, too. Thank You for forgiving me. Please live in my heart so everyone will know."

* Cue music.

[Choir: INTO MY HEART]

SCENE SIX
The Classroom

Kelsey: (continuing) **So, now I'm a Christian, and I'm different than before!**

Boy 3: **You don't <u>look</u> different.**

Kelsey: (smugly) **Well, I am.**

Boy 3: (stubbornly) **I don't <u>see</u> anything different about you.**

Boy 2: **Your hair's the same.**

Girl 1: **Your face is the same.**

Girl 2: **You sound the same.**

Kelsey: (angrily stamping her foot) **Well, I'm <u>not</u> the same!**

Boy 1: **You sure <u>act</u> the same!**

Everyone laughs, except Kelsey.

Boy 3: **I don't think you're really a Christian. Christians are supposed to be sweet and nice.**

Kelsey: (blowing her top) **I AM <u>TOO</u> A CHRISTIAN!**

Everyone laughs, except her.

Mrs. Bowen: (kindly, trying to ease the situation, putting her arm around Kelsey) **Kelsey, I think the kids have a point. It's not enough just to <u>tell</u> them Jesus lives in your heart. You have to <u>show</u> them, too.**

Kelsey: **Well, how can I do that? That's on the inside.**

Mrs. Bowen: **You show what happened to you <u>inside</u> by the way you act on the <u>outside.</u>** (to class) **What are some ways Kelsey could show us on the outside what's happened to her on the inside?**

Boy 1: **Be kind.**

Girl 1: **Be a good friend.**

Girl 2: **Tell the truth.**

Boy 2: **Help people.**

Girl 3:	**Share.**
Boy 3:	**And quit yelling so much!**

All laugh. Cue music.

Mrs. Bowen:	**If you're different on the inside, your life will show it on the outside.**

[Choir: IF YOU'RE HAPPY AND YOU KNOW IT]

SCENE SEVEN
Outside after School

Kelsey is talking with Girls 1 and 2. Lauren enters.

Lauren:	**Well, Kelsey, how did it go with Show and Tell?**
Kelsey:	**Oh . . . not so great, I guess.**
Girl 1:	**Oh, I don't know . . . I learned how Jesus told us God loves us by showing us on the cross.**
Girl 2:	**And I learned how to ask Jesus to live in my heart.**
Kelsey:	**And I learned that if you want to tell people about Jesus, you better not yell at them!**

They laugh, and exit together.

VO Kelsey:	**Well, that's what happened my first day as a new Christian. Like I said, it wasn't exactly what I had planned. I'm still so excited about having Jesus in my heart that I can't wait to tell everyone about it. But I guess I'll just have to work on the "show" part! *Good night, Diary. Isn't knowing Jesus just wonderful?**

*Cue music.

[Choir: BLESSED ASSURANCE]

THE END

CHRIST THE LORD IS RISEN TODAY
Musical #4

Synopsis

The children in Mrs. Stark's Sunday school class have come on Easter Sunday morning with Easter baskets. Mrs. Stark has her own Easter basket, which is full of unusual Easter symbols. As Mrs. Stark explains each one, the children make the symbols for their own baskets, learn the story of Easter, and discover there's more to Easter than eggs and bunnies.

Song Titles

Opening ....He Lives
Scene One ....Behold, What Manner of Love
Scene Two ....Ho-ho-ho-hosanna
Scene Three ....When I Survey the Wondrous Cross
Scene Four ....There Is a Savior
Scene Five ....Christ Arose
Scene Six ....He Is Lord
Scene Seven ....Christ the Lord Is Risen Today

Set

Option A

Children's choir is placed on risers to the right and left of centerstage. Upstage center, between the risers is a bookshelf, with Sunday school supplies, books, etc. on the shelves, and the top shelf cleared; this is where the children will place their Easter baskets when they enter.

Down center is a Sunday school table and five chairs. (See placement of chairs in the diagram on next page.) In the center of the table are crayons, scissors, glue, glitter, etc. to make the symbols. To the right or left, slightly upstage, should be a teacher's table and chair. On this table are the construction papers and other materials Mrs. Stark will be handing out, and Mrs. Stark's Easter basket.

During songs, the actors can work on their symbols, etc., and the choir stands to sing. During scenes, the choir can sit on risers and watch. This may be enhanced by lighting the Sunday school area during scenes and bringing down choir lighting; vice versa during songs.

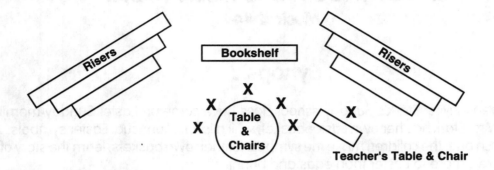

Option B

Choir is placed on steps or risers at front centerstage. Sunday school area is set up as described above in Option A, and played in a platform area to either the right or left of stage. See diagram below. Actors and choir will participate in scenes/songs as described in Option A. (See above also for lighting suggestions.)

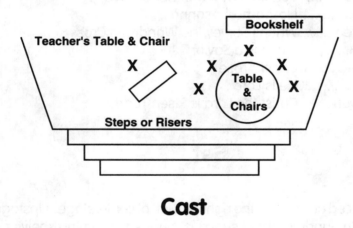

Cast

Mrs. Stark	The Sunday school teacher: may be any age.
Kevin	The children in Mrs. Stark's class.
Jason	
Stacy	
Anna	
Lindsay	

All characters should be dressed in Easter Sunday church clothes. Children enter carrying their Easter baskets. They may also bring Bibles, purses, offering envelopes, etc.

Props

• Five children's Easter baskets (2 boys/3 girls)

• Mrs. Stark's Easter basket (decorated nicely, with a large bow, handpainted eggs, a small stuffed-animal Easter chick, and one sample of each of the symbols the children will be making: a heart, a palm branch, a cross, a candle, a stone, and a crown.)

- 1 Sunday school-room bookshelf, with typical Sunday school supplies, books, puzzles, etc. on the shelves.

- 1 Sunday school table and 5 chairs.

- 1 Teacher's table and chair.

- Art materials on children's table: crayons, markers, scissors, glue, glitter, etc.

- Activity materials on teacher's table: 5 pieces each of red, green, and white construction paper; 5 sheets of gold foil paper; 5 small white candles; 5 stones.

- 1 small, cross-shaped bookmark, wrapped up as a gift.

Script

OPENING

Choir enters and takes their places on steps/risers. Choir may be dressed in Easter Sunday clothes also, or you may choose a uniform of your own design.

[Choir: HE LIVES]

SCENE ONE

Following opening song, choir is seated. Mrs. Stark enters, and begins to lay out pieces of red construction paper at each place. Kevin, Jason, Stacy, and Anna enter, laughing and talking, carrying their Easter baskets. Mrs. Stark crosses to greet them.

Mrs. Stark:	**Good morning, boys and girls! Happy Easter!**
Kids:	**Happy Easter!**
Mrs. Stark:	**Did you all bring your Easter baskets for the Easter egg hunt after lunch today?**
Kids:	(ad lib) **Yes, ma'am . . . sure did . . . Here's mine! . . . etc.**
Mrs. Stark:	**I'm so glad, because we're going to add some things to your baskets this morning.**
Stacy:	**We <u>are</u>?**
Mrs. Stark:	**Yes!**
Kevin:	**What things?**

Mrs. Stark:	Oh, you'll find out in just a moment. Let's set our Easter baskets here on the shelf so we can get to work. (They move to do this)
Mrs. Stark:	(to Anna) **Anna, what a pretty Easter dress!**
Anna:	(proudly) **Thank you! My sister has one just like it. And we have new shoes just alike, too.** (She displays her shoes, and Mrs. Stark exclaims over them.)
Jason:	**My mom made me wear a new suit and a tie. And it <u>bugs</u> me!**
Mrs. Stark:	(laughing) **Yes, I see all of you have new things. It's nice to have new things at Easter. It's sort of . . . symbolic.**
Kevin:	**What's "sym-bol-ic"?** (he hesitates over the unfamiliar word.)
Mrs. Stark:	**A word or picture that represents something, or reminds us of something. Every special holiday has symbols that remind us of its special meaning.**
Stacy:	**Like a Christmas tree?**
Mrs. Stark:	**Exactly.**
Anna:	**Or an Easter egg!**
Mrs. Stark:	**An Easter egg is a beautiful symbol – an egg is a symbol of new life.**
Jason:	**Well . . . what are <u>new clothes</u> a sign of?**
Kevin:	**My mom says they're a sign I've grown another three inches!**
	(All laugh.)
Mrs. Stark:	**That's probably true, Kevin! But I think the new clothes, like the new flowers outside, and the new little baby bunnies and chicks make us think of the new life Jesus brought us when He rose on Easter morning. That's what we're going to talk about today. Stacy, would you bring <u>my</u> Easter basket? It's right over there.**
	(She points to the basket on the teacher's table. Stacy brings it to her, and everyone examines it, ad libbing "Wow! . . . That's pretty . . . Look at that!," etc.)
Anna:	**That's beautiful, Mrs. Stark.**
Mrs. Stark:	**It is pretty, isn't it? A special friend of mine made it for me. She hand-painted these beautiful eggs. And my nephew sent me this cute little chicken.**
Jason:	**But what are all those other things in the basket?**

Musical #4

Mrs. Stark:	**Those are very special symbols of Easter. We're going to make some for each of your baskets this morning.**
Kevin:	(pulling a red paper heart out of the basket) **A red heart? For Easter? This looks more like a Valentine to me!**
Mrs. Stark:	**In a way, Easter is a Valentine.**
Kids:	**Huh?**
Mrs. Stark:	**Easter is God's Valentine to us. At Easter, God showed the world how much He loves us. Kevin, there's a Bible verse on the back of that heart. Can you read it to us?**
Kevin:	(turns over heart and reads) **"John 3:16. For God so loved the world that He gave His only Son, that whoever believes in Him will not perish but have everlasting life."**
Anna:	**We learned that in Bible School!**
Mrs. Stark:	**That's right . . . and what did you learn that it means?**
	Several kids raise their hands eagerly, ad libbing "I know, I know!"
Mrs. Stark:	**Stacy?**
Stacy:	**God loved us so much He sent Jesus to die for us. If we believe in Jesus, He can live in our hearts and forgive our sins. And we can live in Heaven someday with Him.**
Mrs. Stark:	**When Jesus died on the cross, God was saying, "I LOVE YOU!"** (She pauses.) **Now . . . why don't you each cut out a red heart and decorate it as a very special Valentine from God!**
	Kids go to table and begin to work. Choir stands to sing.

[Choir: BEHOLD, WHAT MANNER OF LOVE]

SCENE TWO

Choir is seated after singing. The kids are finishing up their valentines. Mrs. Stark is seated at the teacher's table.

Mrs. Stark:	**If you've all finished your hearts, we're ready to make the next Easter symbol. Jason, come here and I'll whisper to you which one it is.**

(Jason crosses to Mrs. Stark. She whispers in his ear. He looks at her, surprised, and she nods. He looks in her basket and pulls out a large green paper palm leaf. The kids ad lib exclamations of surprise.)

Anna: **A leaf?**

Mrs. Stark: **Not just any leaf . . .**

Stacy: **A palm branch!**

Mrs. Stark: (surprised) **Why, yes, Stacy. How did you know?**

Stacy: **From my friend Leslie. She got to wave one in the Easter pageant at her church.**

Jason: **I saw that! Jesus came riding down the aisle on a <u>real donkey!</u>**

Kids: **Cool!**

Jason: **And the people were waving those branches and singing.**

Kevin: **Singing what?**

Jason: **Uh . . . I don't remember. Something like . . . "ho"** (he stops)

Kevin: **Ho-what?**

Jason: (trying to remember) **Ho-. . .**

Mrs. Stark: **That's right, Jason.**

Jason: **Ho-. . .** (he shakes his head)

Stacy: **Try to remember!**

Jason: (jumping up, remembering) **HOSANNA!***

The kids cheer.

Mrs. Stark: **That's just how it happened. It was Passover, a Jewish celebration. Jesus came riding into Jerusalem on a donkey, and the people lined the streets, welcoming Him, waving palm branches and singing, "Hosanna!"**

*Cue intro. The choir stands to sing. Kids go to table, Mrs. Stark passes out the green construction paper, and they work on their palm branches. A nice touch would be for the choir to have paper palm branches that they wave during the song.

[Choir: HO-HO-HO-HOSANNA]

SCENE THREE

Choir is seated after singing. Kids at table are admiring their finished palm branches, waving them. Lindsay enters shyly, carrying her Easter basket and a small gift.

Mrs. Stark: (looks up, sees Lindsay, and crosses to her) **Lindsay! Happy Easter! I'm glad you're here!**

Lindsay: **I'm sorry I'm late, Mrs. Stark. My mom made us take pictures before we came!**

Mrs. Stark: **It's okay. Let's put your basket here with the others.**

She sets Lindsay's basket on the shelf. Lindsay holds up a small gift and gives it to Mrs. Stark.

Mrs. Stark: **Why, how pretty! Is this for me?**

Lindsay nods.

Mrs. Stark: **Thank you, Lindsay.**

The others turn to see.

Kevin: **Open it!**

The others agree. Mrs. Stark opens the gift. She holds up a cross-shaped bookmark. Everyone "oohs" and "ahs."

Mrs. Stark: **How lovely.**

Lindsay: **It's a cross. For Easter.**

Mrs. Stark: **It's beautiful. And we were just about to talk about the cross.** (She crosses to her teacher's table.) **I'm going to put this special cross in my Bible. And now each of you can make one of your own.** (She passes out white paper.) **Can anyone tell me why the cross is a symbol of Easter?**

They raise their hands eagerly.

Mrs. Stark: **Jason?**

Jason: **Because Jesus died on a cross.**

Mrs. Stark:	Yes, that is how He died; nailed to a cross, on a hillside, like a criminal. It was a terrible way to die. (She says this sadly.)
Anna:	Why did Jesus die that way? He was so good.
Mrs. Stark:	He died to show everyone God loves them. And He died so God could forgive the things we do wrong. *That's why the cross is such a special symbol to believers. It reminds us of God's love and forgiveness.

*Cue intro. Choir stands to sing. Kids remain at table, working on their crosses.

[Choir: WHEN I SURVEY THE WONDROUS CROSS]

SCENE FOUR

Choir is seated after singing. Kids have finished their paper crosses. Kevin and Jason are looking at Mrs. Stark's basket.

Kevin:	Hey! There's a candle in your Easter basket, Mrs. Stark!
Mrs. Stark:	There sure is.
Jason:	How did <u>that</u> get in there?
Mrs. Stark:	I put it in there. It's one of my Easter symbols.
Anna:	A candle is an Easter symbol?
Mrs. Stark:	A candle reminds me that Jesus is the Light of the World.
Lindsay:	What does that have to do with Easter?
Mrs. Stark:	(thinking) Well . . . are you ever afraid of the dark?
Kids:	Yes!
Mrs. Stark:	And what helps you to not be afraid?
Lindsay:	My mom leaves the bathroom light on.
Anna:	I have a Care Bear nightlight.
Kevin:	I have a flashlight.
Mrs. Stark:	And having that little light makes the darkness not-so-scary, right?

Kids:	**Right.**
Mrs. Stark:	**In just the same way, Jesus helps us when we are afraid. He is our Savior from our sin. But He is also our Savior from our problems and fears.**
Stacy:	**That reminds me of my favorite Bible verse: "When I am afraid, I will trust in You."**
Mrs. Stark:	**That's perfect, Stacy. Let's all say that together.**
Kids:	**"When I am afraid, I will trust in You."***
Mrs. Stark:	**Stacy, let's give everyone a candle for their basket.**

*Cue intro. Choir stands to sing. Stacy and Mrs. Stark give out candles.

[Choir: THERE IS A SAVIOR]

SCENE FIVE

Choir is seated after singing. Kids put their candles with their other symbols. Jason is still looking at Mrs. Stark's basket.

Jason:	**Now, I <u>know</u> you didn't mean to have <u>this</u> in your basket!**
Lindsay:	**What is it?**
Jason:	(holding it up) **A rock!**
	The kids laugh.
Anna:	(laughing) **Maybe she ran out of Easter eggs!**
Stacy:	**That's the strangest egg <u>I've</u> ever seen!**
Mrs. Stark:	**Laugh all you like . . . but that stone happens to be my favorite Easter symbol.**
Kevin:	**You've <u>got</u> to be kidding. A rock is an Easter symbol?**
Lindsay:	**You've got us there, Mrs. Stark. You'll have to explain.**
Mrs. Stark:	**After Jesus' death, the disciples buried Him in a tomb. The government had a huge stone rolled across the entrance, so they could be sure He was sealed away for good.**
Jason:	**That's what <u>this</u> stone is for?**

Mrs. Stark:	**Yes! Easter Sunday morning, when Mary and the other women came to the tomb, the stone had been rolled away! And an angel told them Jesus had risen from the dead!**
Kids:	**Wow!***
Mrs. Stark:	**They hurried back to tell the others the amazing news.**

*Cue intro. The choir stands to sing.

[Choir: CHRIST AROSE]

SCENE SIX

Choir is seated after singing.

Jason:	**I want a rock for <u>my</u> basket!**
Kids:	(ad lib) **Me, too! . . . I want one . . . etc.**
Mrs. Stark:	**I have one for each of you, on the table.**

They go to the table, and pass around a jar full of stones, each picking one. Mrs. Stark begins to pass out the gold paper.

Lindsay:	**What's this gold paper for?**
Mrs. Stark:	**It's to make another symbol . . .** (holds up example) **a crown!**

Kids "ooh" and "ah."

Anna:	**Is the crown for Jesus?**
Mrs. Stark:	**Yes! It reminds us that Jesus now reigns in Heaven with God, His Father. He is not only our Savior; He is our Lord.**
Lindsay:	(cutting out her crown) **I'm going to make Him the most beautiful crown ever.**
Anna:	**What do you think His crown looks like?**
Mrs. Stark:	**We don't know. But we <u>do</u> know that one day everyone will see Him and will bow down to Him as their Lord.***

*Cue intro. Choir stands to sing. Kids remain at table, making crowns.

[Choir: HE IS LORD]

SCENE SEVEN

Choir is seated after singing. Kids have their Easter baskets at the table and are arranging their new symbols in the baskets.

Kevin: **Wow! My basket really looks great with all this stuff in it.**

Lindsay: **I can't wait to show my mom!**

Stacy: **I can't wait to show my little sister!**

Mrs. Stark: **Each of you can show them the symbols we've made:**
– the heart, reminding us of God's love
– the palm branch, and the crowd singing "Hosanna"
– the cross, where Jesus died to forgive us
– the candle, because our Savior is our Light
– the stone, to remind us that He lives
– and the crown, for Jesus is Lord.

Anna: **You know, when you understand the real story of Easter, then Easter eggs and bunnies aren't the symbols of Easter at all!**

Mrs. Stark: **Those things are <u>fun</u> . . . but you're right, Anna. The real symbols of Easter mean a whole lot more. And when you understand them, then you really have something to celebrate!***

Jason: **It's time for church. Let's go, Lindsay. "Bye, Mrs. Stark! See you at the Easter egg hunt!"**

Mrs. Stark: **'Bye, kids! And Happy Easter!**

*Cue intro. Kids exit, calling "Happy Easter." Choir stands to sing. Mrs. Stark and kids may re-enter and join on the last verse.

[Choir: Finale – CHRIST THE LORD IS RISEN TODAY]

THE END

IN THE LORD'S ARMY
Musical #5

Synopsis

Billy, a boy of about 7, loves to play soldier; in fact, he imagines it would be great to be a soldier. He even prays about it at bedtime one night, and gets a surprising visit from an angel, with a message from the Commander-in-Chief. Billy is about to get his first assignment as a soldier in God's army, and it is not at all what he expected. By listening in on Billy's conversation with the messenger, we learn how we can have a part in advancing God's kingdom.

Song Titles

Opening .... I'm in the Lord's Army
Scene One .... Beloved
Scene Two .... Amazing Grace
Scene Three .... O, How I Love Jesus
Scene Four .... No Way! We Are Not Ashamed
Scene Five .... My Turn Now
Scene Six .... What a Mighty God We Serve

Cast

Billy — A 5–7 year old boy, who loves to play soldier.

Joshua — God's messenger; may be played by a boy 4th—6th grade, or by a teen-ager.

Billy's Mom — Voice offstage

Dream Players — Choir members who improvise their parts, providing the combat ambience of Billy's dream;
Jet ("Beloved");
Platoon Leader;
Reporter;
Paul;
Assorted soldiers, airplanes, teletypers, marching troops, guerilla fighters

Set, Props and Costumes

Set

Billy's bedroom. Small area for drama played to one side of the stage, with Billy's bed, bedside table and lamp, small area rug, and an array of small military toys.

Props

Joshua's clipboard, bugle, and map
Paul's pen and paper
Assorted military props for the choir

Costumes

Billy   Dressed in pajamas and robe.

Joshua   Dressed in army fatigues, combat boots.

Dream Players   Their costumes may be suggested by one piece, like a hat or goggles, or a prop, like a toy weapon.

Choir   May be dressed in basic fatigues, available from an Army surplus store; or solid army green t-shirts and khaki pants; or solid colored sweats with military suggestions, such as helmets, goggles, etc.

Script
OPENING
[Choir: I'M IN THE LORD'S ARMY]

SCENE ONE
Reveille

As the scene opens, Billy is sitting on the floor by his bed, surrounded by "GI Joe" type army toys (soldiers, vehicles, etc.). He has arranged them in a scenario and is making the appropriate noises, acting out his battle. His mother speaks from offstage.

Mom/VO: **Billy! I thought I told you to go to bed!**

Billy: (with disappointment) Yes, ma'am.

Mom/VO: **Did you brush your teeth?**

Billy: (climbing into bed, pulling up the covers) Yes, ma'am!

Mom/VO: Did you say your prayers?

He sits up in bed, folding his hands and closing his eyes.

Billy: Okay. Now I lay me down to sleep. I pray the Lord my soul to keep. *(he yawns, continues sleepily)*

Billy: God bless Mommy and Daddy and Sarah. God bless Mrs. Wright at school. *(he yawns, even sleepier, and lies back down, drifting off as he's praying)*

Billy: God bless my granddad, and help him to get well.

Pause. Then, he rouses slightly, sits up again.

Billy: Oh, and God, if you can, please make me a soldier. That would be real neat. *(he lies back down, dreamily)*

Billy: Amen.

Pause. He snores. Several choir members enter and circle his bed, some pretending to be fighter airplanes, some pretending to be soldiers in combat. They make appropriate battle noises as they circle his bed, enacting his dream. Joshua enters, carrying a clipboard and a bugle. He walks through the middle of the "dream," ignoring the actors, and bends over Billy's bed, looking at him. Then he checks his clipboard and nods.

Another soldier: Yep, Joshua . . . that's him.

Joshua: Okay, here goes . . .

Joshua stands up straight and blows "Reveille." Billy sits up straight in bed, startled and disoriented. As he awakes, the "airplanes" fly off, followed by the combat soldiers.

Billy: What was that?

Joshua: Your wake-up call!

Billy: My what?

Joshua: It's time to get up!

Billy: Get up?

Joshua: Fall in!

Billy: Fall in?

Joshua: Report for duty!

Billy: Wait a minute! What's going on here?

Joshua: Billy Cooper, you're being enlisted!

Billy: Enlisted!

Joshua: That's right. Called up. Deployed. Activated. Billy Cooper, God has heard your prayer. You're going to be a soldier!

Billy: Really? A soldier? Like G.I. Joe?

Joshua: Not exactly. More like . . . Gideon.

Billy: Gideon?

Joshua: David!

Billy: David?

Joshua: (proudly) Joshua!

Billy: I never heard of any of these guys.

Joshua looks mildly offended, but Billy doesn't notice.

Billy: Who are they?

Joshua: Only some of the greatest heroes of all time!

Billy: Really? Were they brave?

Joshua: Very brave.

Billy: Did they fight battles?

Joshua: Great battles. And you, Billy Cooper, are being called to join them in the service of the greatest Commander-in-Chief in the universe. You're being called into God's army!

Billy: God? God has an army?

Musical #5

Joshua: **Affirmative! How do you think He accomplishes His plan of action?**

Billy: **I . . . didn't know He had a plan of action.**

Joshua: (as if telling important military secrets) **Operation Redemption!**

Billy: (with awe) **What is it?**

Joshua: **Rescuing the fallen human race from its sinful condition. Restoring them to their original intended purpose for fellowship with God and cooperation in the work of His kingdom. Redemption and Restoration . . .That's His plan of action.**

Billy: (not comprehending) **Huh?**

Joshua: **And you, my friend, are being deployed on a special mission.**

Billy: **Me?**

Joshua: **Isn't that what you asked for? Didn't you enlist? Didn't we hear you pray, "Make me a soldier"?**

Billy: **Yeah.**

Joshua: **Well, consider yourself now on active duty.**

Billy: **Wow! Active duty!**

Joshua: **That's right, and I'm here to begin briefing you on your mission.**

Billy: **Cool!**

Joshua: **What I'm about to tell you is classified information, strictly given on a need-to-know basis. Should this information fall into the hands of the enemy, it could be used against us.**

Billy: **This is so tough!**

Joshua: (overly serious) **On this mission, you'll be employing the use of a secret weapon.**

Billy: **Wow! A secret weapon! Is it a stealth bomber?**

Joshua: **No.**

Billy: A commando sting-ray, fully automatic, sonar rocket launcher?

Joshua: Uh ... no.

Billy: What?

Joshua: Love.

Billy: Love? What kind of weapon is that?

Joshua: (quoting) "The weapons of our warfare are not of the flesh, but divinely powerful for the destruction of fortresses." 2 Corinthians 10:4. It's in the training manual. (explaining) It's true that we're human, but we use God's mighty weapons, and one of the mightiest is love. (quoting again) "Proverbs 10:12: Love covers all sins. 1 Corinthians 13:8: Love never fails. 1 John 4:18: Perfect love casts out all fear." Read the manual.

Love is at the top of God's list on His plan of action. "This is My commandment," He said, "that you love one another." Love can break down any walls. It can overcome any defenses. It is our best action and our best defense. It is the one thing our enemy cannot overcome. Love is our Commander-in-Chief's secret weapon. "Beloved," He told us, "let us love one another."

[Choir: BELOVED]

SCENE TWO
A Winning Strategy

After the song, "Jet" circles Billy and Joshua as they sit on the edge of the bed.

Jet: Commander 1, Commander 1, this is Beloved. Coming in for a landing. Repeat. Coming in for a landing.

Jet, making appropriate landing noises, circles the set and skids to a stop on his knees just outside the set, then exits quietly as drama resumes. Billy is on his knees at the end of the bed, pretending to be a jet himself. Joshua checks his clipboard.

Joshua: Continuing our briefing ... (Billy is not paying attention) Attention, soldier!

Billy snaps to it, stands up on the bed, saluting. Joshua returns the salute and Billy plops down on the bed beside him.

Joshua: Continuing our briefing, . . . I have been authorized to apprise you of the current status of our military operation.

Billy: Huh?

Joshua: I'm supposed to tell you how the war's going.

Billy: Oh! How's it going?

Joshua: We won.

Billy: We won? You mean the war's over?

Joshua: Affirmative, soldier. Mission accomplished. Enemy defeated. Victory for our side.

Billy: How?

Joshua: Propitiation. (Billy looks confused)

Joshua: The Battle of Calvary. You see, our Commander knew that His soldiers could never stand against the enemy on their own, so He sent in His most valiant warrior to do battle for us.

Billy: Who?

Joshua: His own Son . . . Jesus.

Billy: Jesus? You mean, like "Jesus loves me, this I know"?

Joshua: Exactly, soldier. An excellent battle song.

Billy: (shrugging) But . . . it's about love.

Joshua: It's about God's love for us. God loved us so much that He sent Jesus to die doing battle for us, and to defeat the enemy for good at His resurrection. In God's battle plan, that maneuver has a name; we call it "grace."

Billy: Amazing!

[Choir: AMAZING GRACE]

SCENE THREE
Propaganda

After the song, a troop of "soldiers" marches through the set, chanting in time.

Platoon
Leader: **This is God's amazing grace ...**

Troop: **This is God's amazing grace ...**

Platoon
Leader: **Jesus died and took our place.**

Troop: **Jesus died and took our place.**

Platoon
Leader: **God's already won the war ...**

Troop: **God's already won the war ...**

Platoon
Leader: **Tell me what're you fighting for?**

Troop: **Tell me what're you fighting for?**

Platoon
Leader: **(count-off) One – Two ...**

Troop: **One – Two ...**

Platoon
Leader: **Three – Four ...**

Troop: **Three – Four ...**

All: **One – Two – Three – Four – One – Two ...**
Three – Four!

They exit as they are finishing the chant. Joshua and Billy are still sitting on the bed. Billy is pondering the idea that the war's over.

Billy: **So, if the war's already over, how come people are still fighting?**

Joshua: **They don't know.**

Billy: **They don't know?**

Joshua: No. Only the soldiers who've enlisted in God's army and have been briefed, like you, know. The civilians and the enemy soldiers ... they don't know the war's over.

Billy: How come?

Joshua: Propaganda. The enemy puts out a ton of it.

Billy: Like what?

Joshua: Like on TV ... movies ... some things you read in books, in the newspaper ... even some things you learn in school.

Billy: School? I thought all the stuff you learned in school was true.

Joshua: Some of it is. But that's what propaganda is ... the enemy's lies which sound like the truth.

Billy: Have I heard any ... propa .. uh .. ganda?

Joshua: (leaning over to Billy) Ever heard the one about evolution?

Billy: Wow!

Joshua: Yep. Anything that makes us believe we're less than we are; anything that says there's no God; anything that makes us think that this life is all there is, or that we're all that matters ... that's enemy propaganda. I bet you've heard a lot of it.

Billy: But why does the enemy want to tell lies?

Joshua: Read your training manual. "John 8:32: You shall know the truth, and the truth shall set you free." Whenever people discover the truth about God's love and grace, they surrender! The war is over! They're free from the enemy's control. He hates that.

Billy: I can imagine.

Joshua: See, Billy, the truth is irresistable. God's love—our secret weapon—is something people really need. They look for it in all kinds of places, always feeling there's something missing. The enemy has to keep people from discovering the truth of God's love, because when they find it, they can't turn it away.

[Choir: O, HOW I LOVE JESUS]

SCENE FOUR
A Mission of Mercy

After the song, the "news team" takes its place in front of the set area, with the "reporter" in the center, and a "teletyper" on each side. The reporter covers one ear and speaks into his hand as if holding a walkie-talkie type of microphone. On each side, the "teletypers" make "radio signal" sounds continuously as he broadcasts.

Reporter: This is your War Correspondent with a late-breaking bulletin. This information just in. The war is over. I repeat: The war is over. Some fighting still remains in outlying rebel areas, due to enemy propaganda. However, we repeat our earlier headline for those just joining us: The war is officially over and victory is declared. You shall know the truth and the truth shall set you free.

They exit, the "teletypers" still signaling. Joshua is still sitting on the bed; Billy is underneath, fishing out some stray soldiers. We see his feet sticking out. He comes out from under the bed as he speaks.

Billy: Wait a minute. (he bumps his head on the bed) Ouch! (rubbing his head) If the war's over, then what kind of mission am I being sent on?

Joshua: A mission of mercy. (he unrolls a map) Although technically the war has ended, there are still some local skirmishes that remain, and the enemy is still holding many prisoners of war captive. Now we've set up some command posts here and here—your church is one of them— from which we can deploy troops into the surrounding area and recover these POWs. According to the duty roster, that is the nature of your mission.

He points to the map.

Joshua: See this red circle right here? That's your school. That is the sector to which you'll be assigned.

Billy: My school? I'm being sent on a mission to my school?

Joshua: Affirmative.

Billy: (disappointed) Aw, I was hoping for something more exciting than that. Something . . . important.

Musical #5

231

Joshua: A good soldier never second-guesses his commanding officer. What may look like an unimportant mission to you could be crucial to the Commander-in-Chief's plan of action. "Isaiah 55:8: 'My thoughts are not your thoughts,' says the Lord, 'and my ways are not your ways.'" It's in the manual; look it up.

Billy: Naw, I'll take your word for it.

Joshua: (checking his clipboard) According to my records, it says that you've been assigned to liberate a certain civilian named . . . uh . . . Preston Pomeroy.

Billy: Preston Pomeroy! That's who I've been assigned to? Oh, no!

Joshua: What's the problem, soldier?

Billy: Preston Pomeroy is the biggest nerd in the class! He's a dweeb, a loser. The last thing I want to do is to be seen with him. Please, can't I get another assignment?

Joshua: According to our records, this assignment is an emergency. This civilian is surrounded by heavy guerilla warfare. His parents are getting a divorce; he's failing in four subjects; his older brother was just arrested for drug possession; he's got no friends, and is considering running away from home.

Billy: I had no idea all that was going on with Preston.

Joshua: Apparently, the civilian is surrounded, cut off from supplies, and is in danger of becoming a casualty.

Billy: Wow, he really needs a friend.

Joshua: Your mission precisely.

Billy: You mean this is where that secret weapon comes in? You expect me to love Preston Pomeroy?

Joshua: This is a tough assignment for a new recruit like you. It's going to require some covert action.

Billy: Huh?

Joshua: Prayer. And you're going to need information from Military Intelligence.

Billy: Who?

Joshua: The Holy Spirit. And another thing—you'd better bone up on the training manual. You're going to need to know the Word a lot better, if you're going to free the POW.

Billy: Oh boy, I don't know. Be friends with Preston Pomeroy, the class nerd. What will people think?

Joshua: That's your battle to face, Billy. Nobody ever said the army was easy. Why, some of our bravest soldiers have had to face real hardships. Like Peter... or Paul. They both went to prison.

Billy: Hanging out with Preston Pomeroy might as well be prison!

Joshua: But they weren't afraid to pay the cost. And they weren't ashamed to be in God's army!

[Choir: NO WAY! WE ARE NOT ASHAMED]

SCENE FIVE
The Battle Is the Lord's

After the song, three soldiers take their place in front of the set. "Paul" lies on his stomach in the center, as if in a foxhole. The other two shoot over him while he writes a letter. As he writes, he reads out loud.

Paul: One hundred and twenty-fifth day on the front lines. Combat continues. We have been beaten, shipwrecked, starved, in danger from robbers. We are afflicted in every way, but not crushed; perplexed, but not despairing; persecuted, but not forsaken; struck down, but not destroyed. In all these things we overwhelmingly conquer through Him who loved us.

The two in combat cease their fire on the last words. The three exit. Billy is sitting on the floor with his back to Joshua, playing with his soldiers, deep in thought. Joshua is watching him.

Joshua: Billy, can I ask you something?

Billy: (still making battle noises as he plays) What?

Joshua: Do you know that God loves you?

Billy: (continuing to play) Sorta.

Joshua: Sorta?

Billy avoids answering for a minute, continuing his play, then finally he bombs a camp dramatically and ends his battle. He turns to Joshua.

Billy: Well, I mean I've been taught that in Sunday school and choir all my life. So I guess I know.

Joshua: Do you believe it?

Billy: Sure, I guess.

Joshua: (getting down by him on the floor) I mean, do you really believe that God cares about what happens to you; that He wants only the best things for you, and that He would never leave you alone?

Billy: Sure, I know that.

Joshua: Billy, it's okay to be afraid of the battle. That's only natural. Remember David, the soldier I mentioned earlier? Remember his battle with Goliath? He was only a little kid . . . just like you. Don't you think he was afraid? But he knew he wasn't alone. He knew that the battle belonged to God, and that God would fight for him. Billy, when God gives you an assignment, He doesn't send you out there alone. You can be sure that He is right there with you all the way.

Billy considers this, thinks it through.

Billy: Now, let me get this straight. I'm going to be a soldier in God's army, on a strategic mission.

Joshua: Affirmative.

Billy: And that mission is to be friends with Preston Pomeroy.

Joshua: Roger.

Billy: And my being friends with Preston is somehow going to accomplish God's plan of action?

Joshua: Operation Redemption. Winning the POW back from the enemy's camp, and setting him free with God's love.

Billy: I'm going to help Preston discover God's love?

Joshua: Exactly.

Billy hesitates, then makes up his mind.

Billy: Well, I said I wanted to be a soldier!

Joshua: "2 Timothy 2:3: Suffer hardships with me, a good soldier of Jesus Christ!"

Billy: And I know that God will fight for me!

Joshua: "1 Samuel 17:47: The battle is the Lord's!"

Billy: And He'll give me the weapons I need to fight with!

Joshua: "Ephesians 6:11: Put on the full armor of God!"

Billy: Okay! I can do it! I know I can!

Joshua: "Philippians 4:13: I can do all things through Christ who strengthens me!" Check it out! It's—(Billy says the rest of this sentence with him)

Billy: . . . in the training manual. I know! I know!

[Choir: MY TURN NOW]

SCENE SIX
Review the Troops

After the song, the Platoon Leader blows his whistle and the entire choir lines up for the Finale.

Platoon
Leader: All right, men! Fall in for formation! Let's march! Hup-Two-Three-Four! Hup-Two-Three-Four!

All march in time as the Platoon Leader chants "Left, Left, Left, Right, Left" underneath final dialogue. Billy stands at attention and salutes Joshua.

Billy: Billy Cooper, reporting for active duty, sir!

Joshua: All right, let's review what we've learned: Who is our Commander-in-Chief?

All: God Himself, sir!

Joshua: What is our plan of action?

All: Operation Redemption, sir!

Joshua: What is our secret weapon?

All: Love, sir!

Joshua: What is our winning strategy?

All: Amazing grace, sir!

Joshua: What is our assignment?

All: Tell the good news, sir!

Joshua: What is our mission of mercy?

All: Set them free, sir!

Joshua: All right then, troops, mo-oove out!

[Choir: Finale - WHAT A MIGHTY GOD WE SERVE]

THE END

DEAR GOD
Musical #6

Synopsis

Mrs. McMinn is teaching her Sunday school class about prayer. She has asked them to keep a prayer journal for a week; each day they are to write down their prayers to God, as if writing a letter to Him. In this script, we eavesdrop on some of the children's letters.

Song Titles

Opening..............Say to the Lord, "I Love You"
Scene One.......God Is So Good
Scene Two......Love Him in the Morning
Scene Three...Jesus, Name above All Names
Scene Four......Awesome God

Cast

Melinda   A girl age 6-12

Kevin   A boy age 6-12

Lisa   A girl age 6-12

Patrick   A boy age 6-12

Set, Props and Costumes

Set

Four areas where monologues are played, require minimal set pieces, just enough to suggest location:

Melinda   Girl's desk or vanity table and chair, with appropriate lamp and "girl things" on desk

Kevin	Small area rug
Lisa	Large, overstuffed armchair, optional side table and lamp
Patrick	Small table or desk with chair, with appropriate boyish lamp and sports mementos; floor littered with wadded-up paper balls and maybe one or two paper airplanes

Props

Notepad or paper and pencil for each actor (*if memorization of these monologues is a problem, simply let each child have a copy of his/her script for reference, as if that is the letter he or she is writing.*)

Pillow for Kevin

Stuffed animal for Lisa

Bible for each actor

Costumes

Melinda	Dressed in comfortable everyday clothes
Kevin	Dressed in pajamas
Lisa	Dressed in nightgown and robe
Patrick	Dressed in jeans or sweats, tennis shoes, baseball cap

Script

OPENING
[Choir: SAY TO THE LORD, "I LOVE YOU"]

SCENE ONE
Hugs and Kisses

Melinda is sitting at her desk, writing a letter to God. As she writes, she speaks the words out loud.

Melinda: Dear God: It's kind of weird to be writing You a letter. I'm used to just talking to You in my prayers each night, and when we say the blessing at dinner . . . and sometimes in church. But I've never written You a letter before.

In Sunday school, we are learning about prayer. My teacher, Mrs. McMinn, said we should write our prayers down, like a letter to someone we love. I said that wouldn't be hard, because God is someone I love. She said, "Melinda, have you ever told God that you love Him?" I said I didn't know if I ever really had.

Mrs. McMinn says it's a very important part of prayer, telling You how much we love You. She called it "adoration." (I'm not sure how to spell that!) I never knew we were supposed to tell You stuff when we prayed; I thought we were just supposed to ask for things. Anyway, in case I've never told You before, I love You, God. If You were here, I'd give You a big hug, just like I give my daddy. That's kind of how I think of You, like a daddy, who loves me and takes care of me.

I'm putting lots of x's and hearts at the bottom of this letter. X's stand for kisses and hearts stand for hugs. That's what I put at the bottom of all the letters I write to people I love. When You see those x's and hearts, You'll know that's my adoration.

Well, good night, God. All my love, x – x – x – x, heart, heart, heart, heart. Melinda.

[Choir: GOD IS SO GOOD]

SCENE TWO
Quiet Time

Kevin is lying on the floor with a pillow, writing his letter to God. He speaks in a whisper as he writes.

Kevin: Dear God: I have to be quiet while I write this, 'cause it's real early in the morning, and nobody in my house is up yet. I like to get up early and be the only one up. The house is so quiet, and I can have some time all to myself. I have four brothers and sisters, as You know, so it's hard to be alone in this house!

Do You ever get time to Yourself, God? I know the Bible says You never sleep, but even if You're up all night, I guess there's always somebody talkin' to You somewhere. That's how it is around here; there's always somebody talkin' or yellin' or playin' the piano or something. It's hardly ever quiet. Don't You get tired of that? I do. That's why I like the early morning.

Mrs. McMinn says that You are always listening to us, whatever time of day we pray. She read us a Bible verse, "Pray without ceasing." She said that means we should talk to You all day long, not just once a day. Is that right, God? Are You sure You don't mind if we talk to You all day long? I wouldn't want to drive You crazy, but I like to know that You're always listening to me, and that I can talk to You anytime. I could ask You for help on a test at school, or when my little brother is buggin' me, and I could talk to You at night when I'm lying in my bed and I sometimes worry about things. That'd be really great. See, even when you live in a big family, a lot of the time nobody listens to you when you talk. So I'd like to talk to You.

He looks up as if he hears a sound, then goes back to his letter.

Well, I gotta go now. My baby sister's awake, and pretty soon everybody'll be up. I'll talk to You again today, though, okay?

Check You later. Kevin.

[Choir: LOVE HIM IN THE MORNING]

SCENE THREE
Beautiful Savior

Lisa is sitting in an overstuffed armchair, with a stuffed animal, writing her letter to God. She speaks out loud as she writes.

Lisa: Dear God, Mrs. McMinn says we could write to You about all the things we like best about You. She said that's called "praise." I know about praise; we do it in church on Sunday morning. But I didn't know we could also praise You all by ourselves.

Do You know what I like best about You, God? It's Your Son, Jesus. Christmas is my favorite time of year, because I like to hear about how Jesus was a little baby, born in a stable. I like to hear how the angel told Mary and Joseph what to name the baby.

Jesus had a lot of names, didn't He? I asked Mrs. McMinn why, and she said that every name of Jesus tells us something different about Him—like Counselor, Bread of Life, or Lord, or Friend.

Do You know what my favorite name for Jesus is? Beautiful Savior. I learned that in a hymn we sang in choir. It makes me think of my own nickname. Did You know I have a nickname? It's what my dad calls me: "Beautiful." Ever since I was a little baby, whenever he sees me, he says, "Hello, Beautiful," or "Good night, Beautiful." I love that name! It makes me feel special.

Is that how You feel, too? Does it make You happy when we call You by Your special names? Is that why You like to hear our praise?

That's really neat. Tomorrow I'm going to find more of Your names in the Bible, and use them to praise You. But tonight, I'm still going to call You by my favorite name.

Good night, Beautiful Savior! Love, Lisa.

[Choir: JESUS, NAME ABOVE ALL NAMES]

SCENE FOUR
You're Awesome!

Patrick is sitting at a desk, writing his letter to God. The floor around him is littered with wadded-up balls of paper. On the desk are several wads also, and an open Bible. Patrick speaks out loud as he writes; at first, he is frustrated.

Patrick: **Dear God, I'm not eg-zak-ly . . .**

He crosses out this word and tries again.

Ex-sack-ly . . .

He exclaims in frustration, wads up the sheet and throws it on the floor. He leans his head on his hand, elbow resting on the desk, and thinks out loud, not writing.

God, I'm not exactly sure how to say this. I'm not very good at writing. And I'm sure not good at spelling!

What I wanted to say to You is that I think You're—well— awesome! I mean, when I think about all the stuff You created . . . How You could figure out the moon and the sun and the planets, and make everything orbit around like it does . . . Wow! It makes me wonder why You bother with a little kid like me. I mean, I'm not really important.

He flips through the pages of the Bible.

Mrs. McMinn showed us some of the Psalms in the Bible. She said a lot of them were King David's prayers, that he wrote them down as poems and songs. Man! I'm sure glad she didn't ask us to write poems to You this week! I could never do that!

Anyway, she said that whenever we can't think of words to talk to You, we can find a Psalm that says it for us, and think about what it means, and read it to You. She called it "meditation."

He turns to the Psalm he has marked.

I found one that says exactly what I think. Listen!

He begins reading from the Bible. After a few lines, Melinda begins reading aloud at her desk, her voice overlapping his and then taking over the reading as he fades out. In the same manner, the reading passes to Kevin, reading his Bible on the floor, and then to

Lisa, reading in her chair. Finally, it passes back to Patrick, who concludes the Psalm.

Patrick: (reading) **When I look up into the night skies and see the work of Your fingers—the moon and stars You have made—** (Melinda begins) **I cannot understand how You can bother . . .**

Melinda: (reading) **I cannot understand how You can bother with mere puny man, to pay attention to him! And yet You have made him only a little lower than the angels, and placed a crown of glory and honor upon his head.** (Kevin begins) **You have put him in charge . . .**

Kevin: (reading) **You have put him in charge of everything You made; everything is put under his authority: all sheep and oxen, and wild animals, too, the birds and fish and** (Lisa begins) **all the life in the sea . . .**

Lisa: (reading) **. . . all the life in the sea. O Jehovah, our Lord, the majesty and glory of Your name fills the earth.**

Cue intro to "Awesome God," as Patrick takes another piece of paper and pencil.

Patrick: (writing) **Dear God, read Psalm 8. You're awesome! Love, Patrick.**

[Choir: Finale - AWESOME GOD]

THE END

CHEERLEADING PRACTICE
Musical #7

Synopsis

Tiffany's family has just moved to a new town, and it's their first day unpacking in their new house. Tiffany is alone in her new room, filled with boxes, feeling discouraged and missing her old friends. As she unpacks, she finds encouragement from a surprising source—the Bible. Tiffany learns (and so do we) the power of the Word to encourage us and remind us of God's love and care.

Song Titles

Opening ....Children, Children
Scene One ....Do You See What Esau Saw?
Scene Two ....Cast Your Burden
Scene Three......His Strength Is Perfect
Scene Four ....The Joy of the Lord

Cast

Tiffany   A girl 6–12 years of age

Tiffany's Mom   A woman 30–40ish

The Cheerleaders: Joy, Hope and Faith; played by girls 6–12 years of age

Set, Props and Costumes

Set

Tiffany's room, an area set to one side of the stage, with bed (bare mattress), desk and lamp, optional area rug; several moving boxes are stacked around; these may also be stacked all over the stage, to create a "moving day" feel to the whole stage.

Props

Pom-poms for the three cheerleaders

Optional pom-poms for choir members

Bible and card in envelope for Tiffany

Other appropriate items that Tiffany may unpack

Costumes

Tiffany	Dressed casually in jeans or sweats
Tiffany's Mom	Dressed for moving, jeans or sweats
Cheerleaders	Dressed in identical cheerleader outfits
Choir	May dress in solid colored sweats, perhaps to coordinate with cheerleader colors.

Script

OPENING
[Choir: CHILDREN, CHILDREN]

SCENE ONE
A Prayer for a Friend

As the scene opens, Tiffany is lying on the bed in her room. She takes a card out of an envelope, and begins reading it. Her Mom calls from offstage.

Mom/VO: Tiffany! Are you in your room?

Tiffany: Yes, ma'am.

Mom/VO: Honey, why don't you start unpacking your boxes? I'm almost finished in here, and I'll come help you in a few minutes.

Tiffany: Okay.

She sits up, looks around her with a sigh.

Tiffany: My room . . . This isn't my room. My room is back in our old house. It has blue carpet, and yellow walls. Not like this. I sure do miss our old house. And I really miss Jennifer.

She studies the card she is holding in her hand.

Tiffany: (reading) Dear Tiff, I'm sure going to miss you. I wish your dad didn't have to be transferred. Be sure to write and tell me all about your new house and especially your new school. I hope you make new friends, but remember . . . we'll be friends forever. Love, Jennifer. Philippians 1:3-4.

She looks up, thinking.

Tiffany: Hmm. I wonder what that verse says. (looking around) I wonder where my Bible is. It should be in one of these boxes . . .

She opens one or two boxes, looks in, and moves to another box. Finally, she pulls out a few items and finds her Bible.

Tiffany: Here it is. (turning to the verse, she reads) "I thank God every time I remember you. Whenever I pray for you, my heart is full of joy."

Joy pops up from the box where Tiffany found her Bible.

Joy: **Joy? Did you say joy? All right!** (she spells out the word with hand motions) **J-O-Y! Joy!** (hands on hips) **That's me!**

Tiffany: **Who are you?**

Joy: (Joy sighs goodnaturedly and repeats her cheer) **J-O-Y! Joy!** (hands on hips) **That's me. The joy of the Lord. Haven't you ever heard of me?**

Tiffany: **Well . . . yeah, but . . . how did you get in here?**

Joy: **The Word of God! When you opened your Bible, you got me. Well, actually, you got all of us.**

Tiffany: **All of you?**

Joy blows her whistle.

Joy: **Ready? Okay!**

She steps out of the box, and begins the cheer. As she says her name, she does a little cheerleading routine, and holds it in place. As each girl joins her, they do the same.

Joy: **Joy!**

Hope: **Hope!**

Faith: **Faith!**

All: **We are with you all the way! Go-o-o, Tiffany!**

After the cheer, they cross to Tiffany.

Joy: **Whenever you read your Bible, the Word of God encourages you, and gives you faith, hope and joy. You might say we're your spiritual cheerleaders!**

Faith: **The Bible is full of stories about people just like you, who got discouraged. But the Word of God encouraged them!**

Tiffany: **I never thought about reading my Bible when I'm discouraged.**

Hope: Oh, but you should! You can read about Daniel's courage. Or Noah's faith. Or Abraham's obedience. And most of all, about Jesus' love. The Bible is the first place you should look when you need encouragement.

Joy: Ready, okay!

They do a cheer.

All: B...I...B-L-E!
Look in it and you will see!
In—the—Bible!

[Choir: DO YOU SEE WHAT ESAU SAW?]

SCENE TWO
Why Worry?

During the song, Tiffany watches the action, as Faith, Hope and Joy sing along with the choir. After the song, the three return to the set with Tiffany, who is looking through her Bible, still not convinced.

Tiffany: Okay, so I'm supposed to find everything I need in the Bible. Is there a story in here about a girl who's moved away from her best friends?

Joy: Actually, the book of Philippians you were just reading is an excellent place to look. It's a letter that Paul wrote from Rome to his friends at home in Philippi, whom he missed very much.

Tiffany: Really? Did he have to move away?

Faith: Worse than that. He was in prison.

Tiffany: Oh. It must be a sad letter. I don't think I want to read it.

Hope: Actually, it's all about joy.

Joy smiles and acknowledges this.

Joy: My favorite book of the Bible!

Faith: Read Philippians 4:6 and 7.

Tiffany: (reading) "Don't worry about anything; instead, pray about everything. Tell God your needs and don't forget to thank Him for His answers. If you do this, you will experience God's peace . . . His peace will keep your minds and hearts at rest as you trust Jesus."

Hope: The Devil wants to discourage you by making you worry about things. But Jesus says, don't worry. Cast your burden on Me . . . I'll take care of things for you.

Joy: That's where faith comes in.

Faith smiles.

Joy: Faith means that you believe that God wants the best for you.

Faith: (putting her arm around Tiffany) Don't worry about your new life here, Tiffany. Remember that Jesus loves you. You've got to trust Him to take care of you here. Instead of worrying, try praying.

Tiffany: Praying?

Joy: (jumping up, the others joining her) Ready, okay?

All: (chanting in rhythm and snapping their fingers)
Hey, everybody, here's a secret you should hear:
If you believe it, all your worries disappear.
Cast all your burdens upon Jesus when you pray.
He's gonna roll those burdens away.
Away! Away!

[Choir: CAST YOUR BURDEN]

SCENE THREE
I Can Do All Things

Tiffany: Well, suppose I pray about it? Nothing's changed. I still have to live in this new place. I still have to go to a new school. I still don't have any friends. And I still miss Jennifer.

Joy: (to Hope) Well, Hope?

Hope: Don't look at your circumstances. Look at God. He's greater than anything you face. Maybe He's not going to take away all your problems. But He can help you live through them.

Tiffany: How?

Hope: Read Philippians 4:12 and 13.

Tiffany: (reading) "I know how to live on almost nothing or with everything. I have learned the secret of contentment in every situation, whether it be a full stomach or hunger, plenty or want, (Hope begins reading with her) for I can do everything God asks me to with the help of Christ, who gives me the strength..."

Hope: (reading with her) "For I can do everything God asks me to with the help of Christ, who gives me the strength..."

Tiffany sighs.

Faith: Let's pray, okay, Tiff?

Tiffany nods, overcome. Joy, Faith and Hope gather around her and pray with her.

Faith: Jesus, I know You love Tiffany. I just ask You to remind her of that. I know that she feels all alone right now. I pray that Your Word will be a gift to her, encouraging her and reminding her that You are right here taking care of her. Give her strength to find a new life, with new friends. (cue intro to "His Strength Is Perfect") Thank You, Lord, for always being with us. Amen.

[Choir: HIS STRENGTH IS PERFECT]

During the song Tiffany continues to pray, as each cheerleader gives Tiffany a big hug and returns to the box she came out of, disappearing.

SCENE FOUR
A Housewarming Gift

After the song, Tiffany's mom enters, wiping her forehead with the back of her hand.

Mom: Whew! That was a job! Ready to unpack your room?

She moves to open the box Joy was in, as Tiffany stands and arranges the open Bible and Jennifer's card carefully on her desk, wiping away tears she doesn't want her mom to see.

Tiffany: **Sure, I guess. I was just getting started.**

Her mom opens the box and pulls out one of Joy's pom-poms, surprised.

Mom: **Now, where did this come from?**

Tiffany crosses to her, taking the pom-pom with a secretive smile.

Tiffany: **Oh, that. I guess you could say it was a gift from a friend . . . kind of a housewarming present!**

There is a knock at the door, offstage.

Mom: **Oh, there's the phone man.** (calling offstage) **Be right there!**

She crosses to exit, turning back just before leaving.

Mom: **I didn't know any of your old friends were cheerleaders.**

Tiffany: **They weren't.** (she grins) **This is a gift from a new friend.**

Mom: (smiling) **A new friend. How nice!**

She exits, as Joy blows her whistle, the intro to "The Joy of the Lord" begins, and the cheerleaders return to lead the Finale.

[Choir: Finale - THE JOY OF THE LORD]
Joy, Faith, Hope and Tiffany lead the others. At the end, all freeze in a finishing pose.

THE END

NATURE WALK
Musical #8

Synopsis

Mrs. Crosby's choir is on a nature walk; but Ashley and Darren just aren't into it. They think it's boring, and don't see what it has to do with singing. When they decide to sit it out, they get a surprising lesson from nature, and we discover some reasons for praising God.

Song Titles

Opening.................Joyful, Joyful, We Adore Thee
Scene One...........Hallelu, Hallelujah!
Scene Two...........The Ducks Go By
Scene Three.......The Butterfly Song
Scene Four..........Fairest Lord Jesus
Scene Five...........He Is Exalted

Cast

Ashley   A girl 6–9 years old

Darren   A boy 9–12 years old

Rose   A talking flower; she is the most outspoken flower, very earnest

Daisy   A talking flower; she is the "daffy" one, a little air-headed; she speaks in a high, flighty voice

Fern   A talking plant; she speaks with a Brooklyn accent, has a very "can we talk" attitude; when she's not talking, she files her nails

Mrs. Waddell	Mother duck; very bossy, speaks in a "snooty" voice, rolls her "r"s and stretches out her vowel sounds; very upper crust
Ducklings	Six–eight smaller children, who "waddle" by squatting while they walk
Tree	A talking plant; minimal lines; should be played by a boy
Rock	A talking rock; has one line; played by boy or girl
All Nature	The choir

Set, Props and Costumes

Set

Area reserved to one side for scenes; minimal set required, just enough to suggest outdoor setting (artificial trees, plants, etc.); bench pre-set in this area.

Props

Two paper bags

Costumes

Ashley	Dressed casually, in school clothes
Darren	Dressed casually, in school clothes
Rose	Dressed in green sweats with Rose flower headpiece
Daisy	Dressed in green sweats with Daisy flower headpiece
Fern	Dressed in green sweats with a leafy Fern headpiece
Mrs. Waddell	She should wear a society hat, high heels, and "old lady" dress with overpadding, and carry a handbag
Ducklings	Dressed in white sweats with optional yellow/orange sneakers; orange construction paper "bills"
Tree	Dressed in green sweats with a leaf hat and circular trunk "suit"

Rock	Dressed in grey sweats with paper "rocks" attached to it (wadded-up grey paper, resembling rocks)
All Nature	The choir should be dressed in appropriate solid colored sweats; flower, tree, leaf headpieces made out of construction paper, with holes cut for their faces to show; "trunk" suits for trees may be made by rolling brown poster board into a tube, and cutting armholes; other birds, butterflies, worms and creatures may be similar, suggested by simple construction paper or flannel costume pieces

Script

OPENING
[Choir: JOYFUL, JOYFUL, WE ADORE THEE]

On the last lines of the opening song, the Tree, Fern, Rose and Daisy enter and take their places on the set. They freeze as song ends.

SCENE ONE
All Nature Sings

Ashley and Darren enter, walking aimlessly, carrying brown paper sacks.

Darren: **There's a bench. Let's sit down.**

Ashley: **Great.**

They sit on the bench, looking weary and bored. Darren drops his paper sack on the ground. Ashley holds hers in her lap.

Darren: **Man, this is boring! A nature walk! What a baby idea!**

Ashley: **I've been on a nature walk before, at Bible school.**

Darren: **How old were you?**

Ashley: **Kindergarten.**

Darren: **See? Baby stuff.**

Rose breaks her freeze and looks at Ashley and Darren, frowning, offended, hands on her hips. Ashley and Darren do not notice.

Ashley: Anyway, who ever heard of going on a nature walk in choir? What does nature have to do with singing?

Rose: (sings from "Hallelu, Hallelujah!," fourth measure of "B" section) Hal-le-lu-jah!

She freezes again.

Darren: What was that?

Daisy: (sings) Hal-le-lu-jah!

She freezes.

Darren: Did you hear something?

The flowers giggle.

Ashley: It's coming from those flowers over there!

Darren: Don't be ridiculous—flowers can't sing.

Rose: Of course we can, silly!

Both kids jump back and exclaim with fear.

Daisy: Haven't you heard the hymn that says, "All nature sings"?

Ashley: Th-that f-flower over th-there s-said s-something!

Rose: Don't you know that Jesus said, "If you don't praise Me, even the rocks and stones will cry out"? That's what's happening here!

A rock jumps up and shouts.

Rock: Praise the Lord!

Ashley and Darren jump in fright.

Rose: See? Silly humans!

Fern: (speaking for the first time) You tell 'em, Rose!

Ashley and Darren jump again, as nature keeps coming to life around them.

Rose: How can you sit there like a bump on a log—

Tree: Hey! I resent that!

Rose: Sor-ry! I just meant to say that if they can't find a reason to praise God, they should take a good look. All nature is singing around them!

Darren: (dubious) Nature is singing?

Fern: Sure. Just listen.

[Choir: HALLELU, HALLELUJAH!]

All nature comes to life as the trees, flowers, rocks, birds, etc. sing their praise. They should stand up and sit down, alternating on the phrases, "Praise ye the Lord/Hallelujah!," as the song is traditionally done. Ashley and Darren watch in amazement.

SCENE TWO
Swimming Lessons

"All nature" sits down and is still during scenes now, but not frozen. After the song, we hear quacking from offstage.

Fern: Uh-oh. Here comes Mrs. Waddell and her big brood of toddler-waddlers. They're always stepping on me!

Mrs. Waddell enters, trailing a stream of small ducklings behind her, who all waddle and quack constantly. She speaks to them as they enter and cross to the others.

Mrs. W.: Come along, children! Don't dawdle! It's bath time; everybody in! Good evening, Rose! Fern! Daisy—Goodness!

She stops short suddenly, causing all her ducklings to bump into each other behind her in a "domino" effect. The last, smallest one bounces off the duckling in front of him and lands on his backside, emitting a small, high "quack!" Mrs. Waddell inspects the two children suspiciously.

Mrs. W.: Who's this?

Daisy: Humans.

Mrs. W.: Re-ally? Are they going to be here long?

256   Musical #8

Fern: Rose is just teachin' 'em a thing or two.

Mrs. W.:   What about?

Daisy: Praise.

Mrs. W.:   Don't they know how?

Fern: They're not very good at it.

Mrs. W.:   Re-ally? (drawing herself up proudly) I'm something of a teacher myself. I home-school, you know. Perhaps I could help.

Ashley: Do you teach your children about praise?

Mrs. W.:   Certainly. I encourage it. Ducks have a lot to be thankful for.

Ashley: (curiously) Really? Why?

Mrs. W.:   (offended) Ducks are one of God's most beautiful creatures. And we are excellent swimmers.

Darren: (not impressed) I can swim.

Mrs. W.:   (scornfully) Oh, re-ally. Can you fish?

Darren: Sure.

There is a long silence. Daisy gulps.

Daisy: Oh, boy.

Mrs. W.:   (with her nose in the air) I suppose you can quack, too.

Darren: Nope.

Mrs. W.:   (dismissing him summarily) Well, there you have it. Come along, children. We'll take our bath elsewhere tonight. I can see there's no point in remaining here. (she looks pointedly at Darren, sniffing haughtily) Anyone who cannot appreciate ducks is obviously—well—quacked!

She exits, ducklings following in tow, quacking.

[Choir: THE DUCKS GO BY]

SCENE THREE
Made in His Image

Darren stands and stretches.

Darren: Ashley, can we go now? This nature walk is getting weirder by the minute. First, I'm talking to flowers; now I'm getting a lecture from a duck!

Fern: Mrs. Waddell can be a little overbearing, but she does have a point.

Ashley: What do you mean?

Fern: At least she knows she's special to God, and thanks Him for it.

Rose: Which is more than we can say for you.

Darren: Excuse me . . .

Rose: Hey! Don't get me wrong. I like being a flower. (sentimentally) Especially a rose . . .

Daisy: Daisies are nice!

Ashley: (politely) They're my favorites.

Daisy: Oh, thank you, dear. How sweet!

Rose: . . . but out of all of us, you two have the most reason to praise God. You're humans! Made in His image! That makes you different from all the rest of us.

Ashley: They're right, Darren. We're the only ones created to be like God. We are very special! That's a great reason to praise Him!

[Choir: THE BUTTERFLY SONG]
Optional solo on first verse by Ashley. During song, the different creatures named are featured onstage.

SCENE FOUR
The Star of Creation

Ashley: Well, Darren, I guess we'd better get back, before the others come looking for us.

Darren: Yeah, besides, we've learned enough about praise.

They move to gather their sacks and leave.

Rose: Hold it! Wait just a minute!

Ashley: What's wrong?

Rose: You're leaving before we've covered the best reason for praising God.

Darren: Which is . . . ?

Rose: Jesus!

Daisy: (with a happy sigh) Jesus! Oh, you're right, Rose. He is the best reason.

Fern: Look around you at God's shining creation . . . the moon, stars, planets—even the sun. Jesus outshines all of them. All the rest of this beauty is just a reflection of His glory.

Rose: So, if you can't think of any other reason to praise Him, think of Jesus.

[Choir: FAIREST LORD JESUS]
This should be sung worshipfully by all, with no detractions in staging or choreography.

SCENE FIVE
Souvenirs

Darren: (checking his watch) Wow! Look at the time! We really do have to go, Ashley!

Ashley: (looking in her sack) But we don't have anything to take back from our nature walk!

Daisy: (plucking a petal from her head) **Here you go, sweetie. Take this!** (sweetly) **To remember me by!**

Rose: (doing the same) **And this!**

Fern: (doing the same) **And this, too!**

Ashley looks up hopefully at the tree, who scowls at her at first.

Tree: (grudgingly) **Oh, all right. Here—**

He leans over so she can pick an "apple."

Ashley: **Oh, thank you! Thank you, all! This has been the best nature walk ever!**

Darren: **And the strangest!**

Ashley: **And we'll never forget what you've taught us about praise! We'll be the best singers in the choir!**

Rose: **Remember, with Jesus in your heart, you'll always have a reason to sing His praise!**

Cue intro to Finale. Ashley and Darren exit, as everyone waves goodbye and "all nature" sings the Finale.

[Choir: Finale - HE IS EXALTED]

THE END

THE KEYS TO THE KINGDOM
Musical #9

Synopsis

In this brief service, we take a look at the "keys to the kingdom"; the Beatitudes.

Song Titles

Opening ....Happy All the Time
Song Two...........Seek Ye First
Song Three.......Like a River Glorious
Finale ....When I Get to Heaven

Cast

Three narrators; may be played by boys or girls.

Set

No set required.

Props

Narrators may read scripts from music stands or podiums, or they may use notebooks.

Script

OPENING
[Choir: HAPPY ALL THE TIME]

Narrator 1: Now, wait just a minute! Jesus didn't say that if we believed in Him, we would be happy all the time, did He? Didn't He say we'd be persecuted? That we'd have troubles?

Narrator 2: That's right. But He did say, "Blessed are you when men persecute you. Rejoice and be glad!"

Narrator 1: Rejoice? Be glad? When we have trouble? What's there to rejoice about?

Narrator 3: We can rejoice because we know what's waiting for us in heaven.

Narrator 1: And, when Jesus comes into our hearts, we can begin to live a heavenly life right here on earth.

Narrator 2: He gave us the keys to the kingdom, found in Matthew 5, 6, and 7.

Narrator 1: "Blessed are the poor in spirit . . ."

Narrator 2: Those are the people who know that they need Jesus. Money or things or power can't buy you eternal life.

Narrator 1: ". . . for theirs is the kingdom of heaven."

Narrator 3: But if you have Jesus as your Savior, you have a great inheritance.

Narrator 1: "Blessed are those who mourn . . ."

Narrator 2: Those who are sorry for the things they've done wrong.

Narrator 1: ". . . for they shall be comforted."

Narrator 3: They'll be forgiven.

Narrator 1: "Blessed are the meek . . ."

Narrator 2: People who don't try to get their own way, but think of others.

Narrator 1: "... for they shall inherit the earth."

Narrator 3: If we trust God to take care of us, He will give us more than we could ever dream of.

Narrator 1: "Blessed are they who hunger and thirst for righteousness ..."

Narrator 2: People who want to be more like God, more than anything else.

Narrator 1: "... for they shall be filled."

Narrator 3: Jesus said, (cue intro to "Seek Ye First") "Don't be worried about what you will eat or drink, or what you will wear. Don't worry about tomorrow. But seek first the kingdom of God, and everything else will be taken care of."

[Choir: SEEK YE FIRST]

Narrator 1: I'm beginning to see how this kingdom stuff works. It's not what happens all around you that matters; it's what's happening inside you. Did Jesus give us any more keys to the kingdom?

Narrator 2: "Blessed are the merciful ..."

Narrator 3: Those who forgive others and show love.

Narrator 2: "... for they shall receive mercy."

Narrator 3: If you forgive others, your Heavenly Father forgives you.

Narrator 2: "Blessed are the pure in heart ..."

Narrator 3: Not people who are just religious, but those who really want to know Him.

Narrator 2: "... for they shall see God."

Narrator 3: God said, "You will seek Me, and you will find Me, if you search for Me with all your heart."

Narrator 2: "Blessed are the peacemakers ..."

Narrator 3: Those who love their neighbors and pray for their enemies.

Narrator 2: "...for they shall be called sons of God."

Narrator 3: Even people who aren't Christians love the people who are nice to them. That's not hard. But only people who belong to God can love their enemies.

Narrator 1: And those are the keys to the kingdom!

Narrator 3: "Therefore," Jesus said, "everyone who hears these words of Mine and does them will be like the wise man who built his house on the rock. And when the storms came, the house stood firm.

Narrator 2: "But everyone who hears these words of Mine and doesn't do them is like the foolish man who built his house on the sand. So when the storms came, his house fell with a great crash."
(cue intro to "Like a River Glorious")

Narrator 1: Jesus didn't say the storms would never blow. But He did show us how to build our lives on the solid rock of His kingdom. So we can have peace, even in the midst of the storm.

[Choir: LIKE A RIVER GLORIOUS]

Narrator 1: Wow! We really can rejoice, and be glad! Even when we have troubles.

Narrator 2: We know that what's going on inside us is forever; what's going on outside us is just temporary.

Narrator 3: We know that God has promised to take care of the needs on the outside, if we seek His kingdom inside, in our hearts.

Narrator 2: We have peace in any storm, because our lives are built on the solid rock, Jesus.

Narrator 3: And we know that someday we will have a great reward in heaven, because we have Jesus in our hearts today.

Narrator 1: So now that you know the keys to the kingdom...rejoice!

[Choir: Finale – WHEN I GET TO HEAVEN]

THE END